THE EXECUTIVE DAD'S PLAYBOOK

The Executive Dad's Playbook

Mastering the Game of Life, Love and Legacy

Sean T. Wheeler

Published by Game Changer Publishing

Cover Design: Skylar Cawley

Paperback ISBN: 978-1-966659-44-0

Hardcover ISBN: 978-1-966659-45-7

Digital ISBN: 978-1-966659-46-4

www.GameChangerPublishing.com

DEDICATION

To my wife Shelli and daughter Sienna, who inspire me to be a better husband, father, and man. To my parents, who showed their love through the time they spent with me and my siblings. To all the husbands and fathers out there who are doing it the right way— making all the sacrifices for their loved ones and living according to a set of principles. To my clients, who've taught me so much about life through sharing their experiences. To the reader, who I hope to inspire to become the very best version of himself and a better role model to those who surround him.

READ THIS FIRST

Just to say thanks for buying and reading my book,
I would like to give you a free gift.
The Secret to Winning the Game of Life—no strings attached!

Scan the QR Code Here:

SCAN ME

THE EXECUTIVE DAD'S PLAYBOOK

MASTERING THE GAME OF LIFE, LOVE AND LEGACY

SEAN T. WHEELER

CONTENTS

INTRODUCTION

This is a book for Executive Dads. It's written for men with children, wives, and families, along with a ton of responsibilities and high-pressured jobs. The pressures of fulfilling all of your responsibilities and obligations between your family and professional career, as well as within your own personal life, can lead you to work excessive hours, feel too stressed out, and ultimately sacrifice time with your family and kids. At the same time, the demands of running a company and being a CEO or entrepreneur can create such pressure on your time that you might end up sacrificing your health and personal relationships. That typically results from neglecting physical activity, failing to maintain a healthy diet, and neglecting sleep. The pressure to consistently perform at a very high level frequently causes men in executive roles to sacrifice time in their personal lives.

Nobody told you that the more successful you became, the more stressful your life would be. They didn't tell you that taking on more projects that generate more revenue would also take up more and more of your time. They didn't tell you that you'd start feeling responsible for the employees or coworkers whose livelihoods depended on your performance. No one told you that you wouldn't be able to enjoy your luxurious vacations because you couldn't turn off your brain, let alone your smartphone. Nor did they tell you that your wife and kids wouldn't give a damn that you brought home millions of dollars a year, and that they'd just be really upset if you didn't help out more around the house. They didn't tell you that all the money, toys, and accomplishments wouldn't make you happy. They didn't tell you that you could be wealthy and successful, but also resented by the ones you love. And I'm very certain no one told you that you could give your kids the best home, food, education, quality of life, vacations, toys, cars, and experiences, but they could also end up anxious and depressed for decades to come. And I think that's incredibly unfortunate. It's why I've created this book.

I'm here to give you a new perspective on what's truly most important in life, based on my 20-plus years of experience as a therapist. I've talked to countless Executive Dads and heard of their struggles, experiences, challenges, regrets, and mistakes. This book will help you to learn from the mistakes of others and avoid the most significant regrets that any successful man could have, all while also ensuring that your children are set up for happiness and success as adults.

I am the Ghost of Christmas Future. I'm going to show you what will happen if you don't change your ways—and it's not pretty. And just like the character of Scrooge from that well-known holiday tale, you'll see how your actions and choices could impact your life, legacy, and loved ones down the road. And if you decide that's not the future you want to create, you'll have the opportunity to change your ways. Now look, I'm not saying you're Ebenezer Scrooge. Most successful men I meet are good men. But there's no better teacher than experience. And you only know what you know. I'm here to help you understand the unforeseen benefits and consequences of your choices.

These 20-plus years of work have taught me that the experiences we have as children have a tremendous impact on how we navigate the world as adults. That impact cannot be overstated. The attention we either do or don't get from our parents cultivates a sense of self and awareness of one's value that has an unconscious but undeniable impact on how we think, behave, and relate to others throughout our lives. I've come to learn about the true nature of human problems over the course of these 20 years while performing more than fifteen thousand sessions with people from all walks of life. I'm very passionate about informing and educating people about the true importance of childhood experiences and prioritizing being a great parent to your child. I do this not only because it benefits you as the parent—just having a wonderful experience of living a life filled with more joy—but also because of the effect your experiences have on how your child grows and matures and lives their life. Again, this effect can't be overstated.

So, who am I? I'm writing to you as an Executive Dad. At the time of this writing, I am the proud father of an 11-year-old daughter. I've been a clinical hypnotherapist for more than 20 years and have been married to my wife for more than a dozen years. Through experience, I've learned to balance the demands of running a business, being there for my wife and daughter, and taking care of myself and my health.

During the first ten years of my career as a hypnotherapist, I had the benefit of learning from other people. I learned from talking to executive men who were decades older than me, as well as others who were just a little further along in life. My wife and I didn't get together until I was in my mid-30s, while many of my clients were men who got married in their 20s and already had a couple of children by the time they reached 30. Many of them became Executive Dads before they learned any of the lessons I was fortunate enough to learn before becoming a father.

While helping these men eliminate stress and bad habits, I learned from the mistakes they made and the struggles they experienced. I learned what choices led to good outcomes and what choices led to bad outcomes. I was lucky to learn so much of that before my daughter was born. Because of that, I knew from the moment she was born what to do and what not to do, and I truly understood the significance of being a great father and creating a balanced life.

I don't claim to be smarter than anybody. I don't claim to be better than anyone. As a therapist, my job is to help individuals become better, not to judge them. I just had the good fortune of stumbling into a career that allowed me to learn a lot about life. A good chunk of that learning prepared me for my role as an Executive Dad. I was lucky enough to learn all of that before my daughter was born. As a result, my daughter has also been very fortunate. She has benefited from the knowledge I brought into her life and the significance I placed on being a good dad for her.

So that's who I am at the time of this writing. I've been an Executive Dad for over a decade now, and I have an 11-year-old girl who is absolutely thriving in all areas of life. Sienna is a piano prodigy. She's excelling at dance. She's doing well with school. Most importantly, she is an articulate and confident kid who easily interacts with other kids and is also very comfortable speaking to adults.

This is a kid who, at age nine, introduced me at a live event to a room full of adult strangers. The following year, she introduced me via video on a giant screen at an event for 150 people, with no hesitation about being seen by all those people. She's brimming with confidence, she's a happy kid, and she's absolutely thriving in life. I know that her life and reality are directly related to the experiences she's had and the care with which her mother and I have raised her.

I'm willing to share anything and everything that's helped me to not only be a great dad for my daughter, not only be the best husband I could be for my wife, but also to take good care of myself. It's easy to focus on bringing home the bacon, earning as much for your family as possible, having a big slice of pie, and enjoying an excellent quality of life. But I've also learned that's not enough. If I'm not in good physical shape, if I'm not rested and properly energized, if I'm not thinking clearly, or if my needs aren't met, then I'm not as good of a father and husband, and frankly, I'm not as good of a therapist as I could be. So, I have also made it a priority to take care of myself and my health. I believe in walking the walk. There's nothing I'm going to tell you that I'm not also embodying and living authentically myself.

So, if you're an Executive Dad, here's what you're going to get from this book: a very clear description of the path that is best for you and your physical health and well-being, the path that is best for your children and your family, the path that's ultimately going to lead to the greatest amount of success for both you and your kids. I will teach you how to do this by helping you balance your life. If you're reading this, your career is likely in pretty good shape (relatively speaking). You're not struggling to keep the lights on. Later in this book, we will talk about the three most important things in life —health, relationships, and quality of life. If you're an executive, chances are you've figured out the money part. (And yes, I understand that just about everyone would like to have more of it.)

We're also going to focus a bit more attention and energy on how we can help you get those other two areas of your life up to the level that would be worthy and deserving of someone as professionally accomplished as you are. As an Executive Dad, your physical and mental health are likely due for an upgrade. So, I will give you some tangible steps to help you improve in those areas. And the other goal is to improve your relationships. Whether that's your relationship with your spouse, your children, or even your neighbors and friends, I'll give you some tangible steps that will help you start taking real action and making changes in how you think, feel, and behave.

I know you're busy, so I won't waste a minute of your time. Every story, anecdote, and perspective shared within these pages has relevance to your situation and potential impact on your life and future (even though the *how* may not always be clear to you at first).

And I'm also going to share with you my thoughts on what some might describe as those big "existential" questions: *Why are we here? What's the meaning of all this?* Because if you're going to organize your life around a set of principles, you should understand the motivation behind them. As a therapist who's learned directly from thousands of our fellow human beings what makes them happy, sad, inspired and fulfilled... Well, I thought it'd be helpful to share that wisdom with you here as well.

But before we begin, I have to mention something unexpected that happened while I was writing this book. I was about 90% done with this manuscript when my wife Shelli was diagnosed with Stage 4 throat cancer. Our family's life was immediately turned upside down. This book, understandably, went on the back burner for about six months. She underwent two months of radiation and chemotherapy. And it was brutal. Cancer is like having an atom bomb dropped on your life. Right at the center of that mushroom cloud was my lovely wife. She had to endure the physical pain and suffering, along with the fear of dying young and missing out on watching her daughter grow up.

I was spared the physical suffering, but had the task of watching Shelli suffer, trying my best to encourage her while considering the prospect of raising our daughter without her. Along the way, my decades-long goal of homeschooling Sienna all the way through high school was shelved as well. Shelli just didn't have the energy to do it when the school year began. So we enrolled Sienna in a hybrid school that she attends three days a week—an option we're grateful was available. We're also grateful for the enormous outpouring of support we received from our family, friends, and community. It was overwhelming. Our parents and family traveled from afar to pitch in all throughout her treatment. As I'm writing these very words, it's been less than a month since we learned that Shelli's tumor is gone and she's cancer-free. She still has a long road ahead, but we're ecstatic that she has gotten an extended lease on life.

And I can tell you unequivocally that the principles I'm sharing with you in these pages were absolutely instrumental in surviving these incredibly challenging times. It wasn't a picnic. It wasn't easy. But I was able to handle it about as well as anyone due to being balanced, level-headed and focused on what was most important in life. Aside from certain brief moments when it's totally appropriate to be nervous or upset (like when hearing for the first time that your wife has Stage 4 cancer), I never became anxious or depressed, and I never lost hope.

After living for nearly half a century a life of relatively good fortune, I finally had my feet put to the fire. And while dealing with those challenges at home, I continued to work with clients and help them with their own challenges. I've developed an ability to compartmentalize my thoughts to such an extent that I can be effective with my present task and address other problems or responsibilities when the time comes. And most importantly, my ability to control my thoughts and emotions allowed me to be the best husband and father I could be for my wife and daughter during the most challenging time of their lives. I don't want to paint a picture of perfection because there were moments when I could have done better, but it certainly could have been a lot worse. What matters most is that my wife is alive, and my family is together while she heals.

And these principles that have been so instrumental to me personally in handling life's challenges and adversity are a big part of what I want to share with you over the course of this book. It's not just about what it takes to be a successful Executive Dad; it's about how to do it.

So, are you ready to become an elite Executive Dad and produce a legacy that will live on long after you're gone?

Let's get started.

CHAPTER 1
MY STORY

f I'm going to listen to someone and take their advice, it's very important to me that they're living by their professed wisdom. It's easy to give good advice, but what's more impressive is when someone actually puts that advice into practice. As a therapist, I've learned that if I'm not actively living in a certain way, I can't congruently give someone else any kind of advice about how to live. If I'm going to help people quit smoking, it doesn't make sense for me to smoke. If I'm going to help people control their alcohol consumption, I can't have a drinking problem. If I'm going to help somebody lose weight, I can't be overweight. So, I learned a long time ago that I have to walk the walk to be effective at what I do.

When I decided to write a book for Executive Dads, I had to do some introspection. I had to ask myself, *Am I really that guy? Am I living my life like I'd want other successful men to live?*

When I learned to do effective therapy, I quickly realized that in order to get people to change, I had to call them on their bullshit. Self-deception is what keeps people stuck. The truth—being honest with yourself—actually sets you free.

So I have an intolerance for bullshit, especially with respect to myself. I can't even say the word "can't" without asking myself, *Is that really true?* Years of meditation instilled an awareness of my internal dialogue that made it impossible for me to lie to myself without realizing it.

So, in response to the question of whether I'm actually living the kind of life I'd encourage others to live, I can answer, without hesitation, "Yes." And no, I'm not perfect. I'm also not an egomaniac. If I had chosen any other walk of life, I wouldn't know what I know. I owe a tremendous debt of gratitude to the sheer benefit of being a therapist. If you've been doing therapy for a living as long as I have, and you've really been paying attention, it's almost impossible not to learn from other people. You learn about what works and what doesn't work. I've taken all that learning, added it to my life, and made improvements in how I live, what I do, and why I do it.

The life I'm living now is one that I genuinely want you to emulate. Here's a brief description of what my current life is like. My wife, daughter, and I recently moved to a new home in Roswell, Georgia. We were already living in Roswell in a house we loved, but we recently discovered, almost on a whim, another house that we absolutely fell in love with. It was designed by an architect who was a disciple of Frank Lloyd Wright. It has big, beautiful windows that look out to a large backyard where our two mini Australian shepherds run back and forth all day, chasing balls, squirrels, and each other. We've been blessed to be able to move into this beautiful house, which some people would call a dream home. We've been able to do this in part due to our ability to bring in enough money to create an abundant life. My wife Shelli has a very successful career and has been excelling since she graduated from college.

I've been able to build the top hypnotherapy practice in Georgia while living a great life and helping thousands of people. We have a wonderful home, live in a great neighborhood, spend a lot of time together as a family, play card games every night at dinner, travel and visit family between four and eight weeks every year, play with our beautiful dogs and cats, and have neighbors who have become good friends. We're very socially active. We're close to our daughter's grandparents on both sides. We have a wonderful, abundant life with our family. We have a beautiful home, pets, and all the "stuff." My wife and I have a marriage filled with mutual love and respect. I help her in every way I can, and she helps me in every way she can.

She manages the homeschooling of our daughter while working from home. My daughter thrives by having her mom at home with her all day. If she needs help with something, Mom is there. We are living what is, in many ways, an idealized life. It's not perfect—no life is perfect. All couples have disagreements, and all parents and children argue at times. That's normal life. But the experience we're having as a family is something I've come to realize is an outlier. Many families, especially those with high-achieving parents, have the wealth and the "stuff." They live in nice houses, have material riches, and take nice vacations. However, one thing we do very well is balance having successful careers with prioritizing and spending lots of time with each other and our daughter.

As I mentioned in the introduction, Sienna really thrives and has greatly benefited from that balance. She sees us every day. We talk to her, listen to what she has to say, and demonstrate her importance to us by spending time with her. Because of that, she's developing exceptionally well. I'm helping my clients transform their lives, doing effective work, and getting great reviews. I've had a waiting list for the better part of a decade and a half. My practice is growing and expanding. I've trained and certified others in hypnotherapy and have hired some of them to work for my practice. I have a virtual assistant, an office manager, and a team of experts helping me grow and scale the business. I work with business coaches of all different types. I have a seven-figure practice.

For the first time in my professional life, I have a tremendous team and a business that is growing and beginning to scale. I'm doing this while working in the office only three and a half days a week. I spend about 34 hours per week in my office, where I see clients and hold meetings. That means I have three and a half days per week at home. Every Sunday, Monday, Wednesday, and more than half of Saturday, I'm at home with my family. Sure, I do some work from home on some of those days. (I'm currently writing this chapter at the Delta Sky Lounge on my way to a conference.) Occasionally, I'll have meetings from home. But still, 80% to 90% of those days off, I'm free. I'm free to play with the dogs, take my daughter out to lunch, and have dinner with my family. I have the freedom and the time to help out around the house, run errands, do laundry, vacuum, and handle other household chores. I'm a normal person and contribute around the home, even as I have created a seven-figure practice that's growing rapidly. I've expanded the services offered to include hypnotherapy certification training. My most recent class had an amazing group of students who had a wonderful time, benefited greatly, and are in the process of starting their own businesses as well.

I'm living the kind of life that some people don't think is possible. Some don't believe it's possible to be a high achiever, earn seven figures, have a thriving business, go to the gym consistently, and spend lots of time with your family, to really have a great bond with them, to have a great social life, and to travel and see loved ones. But I am living proof that this type of balance is possible. At my recent doctor's visit, I saw the results of my blood work—everything was good. And I hadn't been to a doctor in years. The approach I've taken to my health and life—creating that balance between health, family, career, and relationships—has played out as well as I could hope. I'm continuing to improve upon that because right now, I'm doing what many of you as executives are trying to do: Work less *in* the business and more *on* the business. I'm working on creating more time for myself and my family and less time doing the delivery and the hard work. I'm making that happen, creating growth without sacrificing my health or precious time with my wife and daughter. So yes, I am speaking from experience, and I'm talking to you authentically as someone who is actually doing all these things I'm writing about, which means it's possible. If it's possible for me, it's possible for you.

Even if, at this point, it may not seem clear how you're going to do it, I encourage you to sit back, relax, be patient, and just keep reading. You'll discover point-by-point how to get from where you are to where I am, how to make all the changes and adjustments you want and need to create greater happiness, greater health, better relationships, and ultimately become the very best father you can be to your kids. So, I want to start with a brief overview of how I got here and who I am. This didn't just happen overnight. As a therapist with over 20 years of experience, I first want to share the importance of childhood experiences.

I've thought a lot about my childhood, my upbringing, how I got to where I am, how I developed the problems I did, and how I overcame those problems. I'd like to start by describing what I was like as a kid.

THE EARLY YEARS

I was born in the suburb of Livonia, Michigan, to two good parents who were middle-class, blue-collar people. My brother and I, and later my sister, had one thing in common when we were born: We were redheads, even though neither of our parents were. My father had sandy brown hair, and my mother always had dark brown hair, but there they were with two freckle-faced boys in the 1970s. My childhood memories are mostly related to having red hair and freckles (and the Irish temper that everyone said went along with it).

My early childhood is filled with memories of spending time with my mom, dad, and brother. We did family things together. We had great holidays. We took trips to Pennsylvania to see Grandma Burke and Aunt Susie. We took trips to Florida to visit Grandma Wheeler and other relatives on my dad's side. I have fond memories of family trips, playing sports with my brother and dad, and doing things with my mom. I had good, close connections and relationships with my family.

At the same time, I also had a lot of fights! When we were kids, my brother and I probably fought every single day during the summer while our parents were at work. I got into fights at school regularly. I'd get into fights on the school bus. I remember being kicked off the bus three times while attending St. Damian Catholic School in the sixth grade. I then attended Detroit Catholic Central High School, an all-male college-prep Catholic school where my uncle (a Catholic priest) taught French for more than 30 years. You'd think Catholic schools wouldn't tolerate bad behavior, but I got into plenty of trouble! We Catholic boys got into plenty of fights. I fought with my friends, I fought with kids I didn't know, I fought with kids at my school, and I fought with kids at St. Michael's, with whom we shared buses.

I have many stories of getting into fights on the school bus or in the parking lot at St. Michael's. I remember fighting with a kid in the back of the bus. He had me in a headlock, and as he was slamming my head against the rear window of the bus, the glass spiderwebbed! (My parents had to pay for the new window.) I got in so many fights in sixth grade that I was ultimately kicked off the school bus and had to ride my orange banana-seat bicycle to school for the rest of the year. At the same time, I also had the best grades of any student in my class. I was an A student and consistently did well in school. My teachers liked me because I followed instructions. But I had a short temper, and it didn't take much for kids to pick fights with me. That remained a problem all through childhood and into early adulthood.

One thing I've thought about a lot since becoming a hypnotherapist is that life is much more difficult for a child who does not have two loving parents. I was spanked at times by my dad. My parents would yell at us at times. While there was sometimes volatility in our home, it never approached anything like abuse—certainly not compared to the stories of abuse I've heard from my clients. The kind of abuse, neglect, or abandonment that many clients report and experience causes so much psychological damage that it can really screw up a person's life for many years. I had a solid foundation due to the presence of two loving parents who were devoted to spending a lot of time with us. I know that my dad was the ninth of ten kids. The way he tells the story, his dad was sort of "over" parenting by the time he came around. Therefore, his dad didn't spend a lot of time with him when he was a kid, and most of the attention he got from his dad was negative attention.

They later patched things up, but my dad moved out of his home when he was around 14 years old and went to live with a friend. He couldn't put up with his dad's negativity and discipline. So, my dad, having not enjoyed that part of his childhood, decided to make a correction. He did something I've since learned many parents have done. He decided to do better with what he felt his own dad didn't do very well—he would spend a lot of time with his kids. So my siblings Kevin, Erin, and I were all fortunate to be a top priority for Mom and Dad. My dad coached our baseball teams when we were kids. He took us to the ball diamond and pitched batting practice to us. He played catch with us. He played basketball with us in the driveway at home. He took us to the movies. He took us to baseball games at Tiger Stadium.

I have a ton of memories of my dad and mom doing things with us and being there for us. I didn't know at the time how important that was. I didn't consciously understand how much confidence that gave us, but that's what it did. When a parent prioritizes spending time with a child, they communicate to that child that they're worth their time. It's something the kid never consciously thinks about or realizes, but it influences and affects them nonetheless.

My dad was a hockey referee for nearly 30 years. He refereed college and high school hockey games and would even take my brother and me with him to the arenas. We sat in the stands and watched our dad skate around wearing his stripes, blowing the whistle, and sometimes getting booed by fans. These are just some examples of the kinds of things dads can do, even when they're working, even when they have responsibilities. For the first 13 years of my life, my dad worked at a dairy factory where they made ice cream and other products. He went on to work at UPS, which was a very demanding and stressful job. He'd often come home stressed out and irritated about work. But in spite of that—despite how hard he worked and how much he worked—he still made time for us.

By the time my sister came along, my brother was on his way out of the house, and I was in high school. By the time my sister was four or five years old, she was basically an only child. They gave her so much time and love. My dad became a dance dad, and my mom became a dance mom. They guided my sister through her career in dance and on into college. A bit older and wiser in their 40s and 50s, they allowed Erin to thrive. She became the center of their universe. They rarely talked about anything or anyone else.

My parents' lives have been defined by their children. They pride themselves on our success. They poured money into our college education when they could have spent it on themselves. Because of that, we've all been able to thrive in careers that we love. Looking back on my childhood, I see how my parents were devoted and dedicated to raising us the right way. I see the connection between the energy they put in, how much love they gave us, how much they prioritized our well-being, and how well all three of us have turned out.

Although I was a late bloomer professionally, I've achieved career success probably far beyond what my parents ever hoped for. My brother and sister are both happily married and doing what they love. My brother has been a radio host for more than 20 years. He's taken great care of his wife and daughter. My sister is a schoolteacher and proud mother of a little girl. My brother has an adult daughter who's college-educated, very intelligent, and on her own path to success. When I look at my own family and those of my siblings, I see the product of my parents' choices. They really prioritized family above anything and everything else. In fact, now well into their 70s, they still do.

Yet, despite that solid foundation from my childhood experiences, I still had my struggles. Frankly, we all do. I was always a pretty shy kid, all the way up to the age of 26 (when I was hypnotized for the first time). Anyone who knew me would know I was very shy and reserved when they first met me. Until I knew you, I didn't feel comfortable being myself. Part of that may have come from the red hair and freckles. I hated my hair so much that I'd wear my baseball cap to bed. Mom would come in after I fell asleep and remove it.

The kid with red hair and freckles gets called "Freckle Face," "Carrot Top," "Strawberry Shortcake," and lots of other names that probably aren't all that bad. But when you're a kid, it can really get under your skin. The awareness of the ways I was different—and perhaps not as popular or as readily accepted into the group as some other kids—seemed to be focused on a bit too much and caused me to struggle with self-confidence into early adulthood. When it came to dating, I had a bit of luck in high school. A friend set me up with a girl who quickly became my girlfriend and eventually my high school sweetheart. I had a fantastic time with her and still have great memories from those days. The not-so-great part was that I was able to get through all of high school without ever asking a girl out. The lack of skill in that area caused some serious problems down the road. My story of heartbreak is relevant because I became known as the *Heartbreak Hypnotist™* due to some appearances on a popular radio show in Atlanta and through the work I did to heal listeners' broken hearts.

The ability to heal broken hearts came in part from my own struggles. When I left my home state of Michigan to attend the University of Miami, my high school sweetheart and I attempted—with great sincerity and naiveté—to maintain a long-distance relationship. She stayed closer to home while attending Michigan State University. It worked pretty well for almost our entire freshman year.

Then things started to go south. Early into our sophomore year, it was over. When she broke up with me, I took it very hard. That amplified my struggle with self-confidence. Until then, my self-confidence was strongly dependent on her love for me. This is something I've talked about with many clients over the years. When your confidence is too closely connected to how someone else feels about you, what someone else says about you, and what they think about you, it's not very strong. Once I lost her affection, my self-confidence crumbled very easily. I spent the better part of the next half-decade being down on myself, struggling with self-confidence, and feeling unhappy. My favorite story from this time was when I took a class trip from Miami to Chicago to visit some television studios as part of my studies in broadcast journalism.

You see, my plan wasn't to be a hypnotherapist. My original plan was to be involved in sports journalism. Like my brother, I loved sports and wanted to be involved in it in some way. I went to the University of Miami because they have a great communications program. (And also because when you're from Michigan and suffer through six months of a long gray winter, being able to wear shorts in January and enjoy palm trees all year is hard to beat.)

While in Chicago, we had the luxury of attending a baseball game at Wrigley Field. The problem was that on this particular April day, the temperature was a frigid 17 degrees. I recall this very clearly because I didn't even have a warm jacket to wear. I remember wearing some sort of tweed sport coat and a sweater while seated somewhere between home plate and third base, shivering with my fellow thin-blooded Miami students. We left after the third inning because we couldn't take the cold anymore, and we walked across the street and through the doors of the first bar we could find. This bar was really jumping, with a live band playing and people dancing. It was very crowded. It seemed like a cool place. But before I knew what was happening, an attractive girl approached me and started dancing in front of me—right in my face. Without hesitation, without even having a moment to think, I looked right at her and said, "What are you, drunk?" She immediately stopped dancing, looked me square in the eyes, and politely said, "No." Then she walked away. At the time, I didn't know what had just happened. I didn't even have time to think.

That's part of the point. When I tell clients that story, I ask them, "Why would I have said what I said to her?" It's a perfect example of how our thoughts influence our perception. The way we think of ourselves influences the way we perceive others and the way we interpret the world. The truth is that I asked her if she was drunk because, in my view, through my own filter, the only explanation that made any sense for a pretty girl dancing with me was that she was too drunk to know any better. She was too drunk to see how worthless or unattractive I was—that's how I thought about myself.

In hindsight, it's a funny story because it's a clear example of someone getting in their own way. But I had many stories like that because the way I was looking at myself was wrong. I was focusing too much on what I didn't like about myself and too little on all the good things I had going for me. This behavior and attitude, and the lousy self-esteem that gave rise to it, stayed with me all the way up until that magical day in January of 2001 when I strolled into the office of a hypnotherapist.

A LIFE-CHANGING DISCOVERY

What's amazing is that my life-altering hypnotherapy session wouldn't have ever happened had it not been for one moment of chance. I have a very good friend who I've known since the first grade. He and I attended school together all the way through the twelfth grade. In high school, we became very good friends. In December of 2000, I was visiting him over winter break in Royal Oak, Michigan. One morning, I was sitting on his couch, waiting for him to get dressed so we could go out for breakfast. Back in the days before cell phones, people sometimes read books. So I looked at his little bookshelf, and one book caught my interest. It was a very thin book about self-hypnosis. I pulled that book off the shelf and read about three or four pages before we left for breakfast. But those three or four pages piqued my curiosity to such an extent that when I came back to Atlanta, I immediately picked up a book about hypnosis. The more I read, the more curious and interested I became. I tried to hypnotize myself based on the instructions in one of these books, but I couldn't really tell that anything happened.

At this point in my life, I was struggling with performance anxiety and social anxiety. The social thing I didn't even quite under-stand, and I knew that performance anxiety was a problem.

I was working at CNN and had an opportunity to do some work on camera. It wasn't the main CNN network but CNN's Airport Network. My broadcast was seen exclusively on overseas flights. But I got an opportunity to be an anchor in front of the camera, delivering a short sportscast. The problem was that I got nervous when I sat in front of the camera, and the teleprompter began to roll. Of course, I wanted to be less nervous. At the same time, my hobby was improv comedy theater. I was taking classes at Whole World Theater in Atlanta, which was the coolest place around at the time. It was always packed. The shows were always sold out. The actors and the people at the theater were the most fun, interesting, and playful people in town. They were smartasses like I was; it was just a great energy to be around. Yet, when I was on stage during classes or rehearsals, the nerves would be so intense that I wasn't able to perform at my best. I desperately wanted to fit in with that crowd. I wanted to be liked! So I put pressure on myself, which actually made things worse.

After trying in vain to hypnotize myself with a book, I made an appointment with a hypnotherapist. A couple of days later, I was at his office and, for the first time in my life, talking to somebody about my problems. I had never done any form of therapy before and had no idea what it was all about, but there I was, talking to Dr. Wesley Anderson, who I will always remember fondly. Wesley passed away in 2019 after a long battle with cancer, and I will forever be grateful to him for changing my life that day in January of 2001. I walked into his office naïve, with the stated purpose of getting some help performing in front of an audience and in front of the camera. However, within a very short period of time, Dr. Anderson picked up on the fact that I was a very negative person. At one point, he asked me a question that caught me off guard.

He asked me to think of three really bad things that had happened to me in my life. Within seconds, I quickly identified three things. Then he asked me to think of three really good things that had happened to me. I struggled to think of even one. And I had a pretty good life! By the time that session was complete, Dr. Anderson had achieved such a profound change in my thinking that I can still remember to this day walking out of his office and down the long hallway to the elevator. During that long walk down the hallway, I specifically recall that I was just walking. I didn't have any thoughts buzzing through my head. My mind was quiet. Normally, there'd be worries and thoughts about responsibilities and money, who didn't like me, and what I was going to do that weekend. But at that moment, I was just walking down the hallway.

I had this feeling of calm and mental clarity that I'd never experienced before. It was profound. I went to Whole World Theater that night. In a room surrounded by the actors and all the other people who worked there, it was a completely different experience from any I'd had before. I had no self-consciousness, nervousness, or anxiety. I was calm, relaxed, comfortable, and present. I knew at that moment that something very significant had changed. I knew at that moment that hypnosis was something I was going to continue. I didn't yet know that it would become my life and career, but I had decided it would become a daily practice.

I got an idea from reading a book before the session. I brought a blank cassette tape to that appointment. I asked Dr. Anderson if he would make a recording of the hypnosis part of the session, and he did. For years, I never went a day without listening to it. Day after day, week after week, and month after month, this new and different experience became the new norm. I became more relaxed and confident. I became happier. I became a better actor. After six years of not being in a relationship, two weeks after my first session with Wesley, I met someone and was very shortly thereafter in a relationship. For the first time in my life, I could talk to a girl I was attracted to without feeling nervous and shooting myself in the foot.

It was effortless to make conversation and get to know her, almost like a dream. It felt too good to be true. But that became the new norm. I became happier socially and personally, more confident, calmer, and more at peace with myself. Within a year, I became not only an actor but also a Master of Ceremonies (MC) at Whole World Theater, taking on the role of directing the actors and hosting the live show. The same guy who had been too nervous to make small talk with strangers was out there week after week, standing on stage in front of a sold-out crowd, hosting a comedy show. I was making people laugh, thinking on my feet, and leading a group of actors in a performance. It's incredible to realize that only one year prior, I was a shy, angry, resentful young man seeing a hypnotherapist for performance anxiety.

Leaps like that helped me understand the profound impact that this hypnosis stuff was having on me. Four years after my initial session with Wesley, I bumped into a girl at the theater. She was a former classmate I hadn't seen since my transformation. After 30 seconds of speaking to her, she held her hand up to my face and said, "Stop," interrupting me mid-sentence. She looked me in the eyes with a puzzled expression and said, "I can't believe you're the same person." She then said, "I used to be afraid of you." That made sense because back in the day, when I was the old Sean, the truth is that I was pretty angry. I wasn't just shy, depressed, or anxious. I was frustrated. That frustration and anger sometimes came out when I was on stage. I had changed so dramatically in my energy and body language that, to her, it looked like a different soul or spirit was inhabiting my body. Although I knew I'd changed, that was a clear reminder of just how far I'd come.

In 2002, I experienced a great misfortune. The network I was working for at that time was sold to ESPN. Several of my peers and I were out of work. I was 28 years old and freshly laid off from my job at CNN. I hadn't expected that. I fully expected to spend my entire career in television doing sports journalism. My hope was to be on air, but I was perfectly happy just to be involved in sports, as that was something I truly loved. But I lost that job and was starting to think about what to do next. I really didn't know. But it did occur to me to consider hypnotherapy. During that time of unemployment, I asked Dr. Wesley Anderson for advice. He recommended that I take in-person hypnotherapy certification training. He said, "I just so happen to know a colleague who runs a course every year, and her next one is starting soon."

So he referred me to Jane Ann Covington, who at the time had more than 30 years of experience as a hypnotherapist. Within a week, I signed up. I put down $3,000 (using a credit card to cover funds I didn't have); I simply knew it was the right thing to do. I was certified in clinical hypnotherapy in May 2003 and immediately started my practice. Over the next four years, between 2003 and 2007, I built my practice part-time while working with Turner Broadcasting System (TBS) full-time. (I had been fortunate enough to get a full-time job later in 2003 that helped pay the bills while I was growing my practice.) In the fall of 2007, I took another leap of faith and let that job go. I decided to put in my two weeks' notice and quit that job to give 100% of my time and energy to my practice and clinical hypnotherapy. Two years prior, I had said a tearful goodbye to Whole World Theater and my love of improv because I knew that I needed to devote more energy and attention to my practice if I was going to make it work.

So that's what I did. 2008 was difficult: I didn't know anything about business, and we were going through a recession. The phone wasn't ringing. I wasn't making much money. But at the end of 2008, I made a solid decision and took a leap of faith. I hired a consultant named Craig Eubanks, who had a website called hypnosis-marketingtips.com. I gave him $450 for a two-hour phone consultation. He gave me great advice on how to grow my business. Starting on January 1st, 2009, my business finally became profitable. At the end of 2009, the universe again gave me an opportunity. I received a phone call from someone with *The Bert Show*, a very popular morning radio show in Atlanta that is also syndicated across the country. They asked me to come on the air and hypnotize one of their hosts, Jenn Hobby, to stop smoking.

I'd never heard of *The Bert Show*, but I knew I wanted media exposure. I knew that more exposure and publicity would be a good thing because I was doing good work and I'd had success with many clients. So I said yes to their offer to go on the show. Although I did not hypnotize her on the air (for safety reasons), I did hypnotize Jenn Hobby in January 2010. She stopped smoking that day. The very next day, on the air, she told hundreds of thousands of their listeners about it, and my business immediately exploded. Within a few weeks, my practice was booked three months in advance. I was doing so many sessions that I was beginning to lose my voice! I had to plan a week off work several months in advance, otherwise I would've been booked up indefinitely. As a result of that one opportunity, my business grew, and I gained a level of prominence that I've been able to maintain ever since.

The following year, I made my first television appearance on *Swift Justice with Nancy Grace*, and a multitude of other good opportunities followed that allowed me to create the premier hypnotherapy practice in the state of Georgia. When I became known on *The Bert Show* as the *Heartbreak Hypnotist*™, that became a big part of my brand for the better part of a decade. It also afforded me the opportunity to learn a lot about marriage and relationships from those who sought my help. And right around that time—in 2013—my daughter Sienna was born.

I met my wife, Shelli, in 2010. We were engaged in 2011. We got married in 2012, and Sienna was born the following year. Now, in the decade since my daughter was born, I've put into practice everything that I'm sharing with you about how to be a great father. I'll show you how to set your children up for success so they won't have to go through the pains, challenges, struggles, and discomfort that I did before my life changed dramatically at the age of 26.

CHAPTER 2
THE EXECUTIVE DAD'S DILEMMA

A t the time of this writing, I have roughly 21 years as a therapist under my belt. Interestingly enough, my daughter Sienna was born right in the middle of those first 20 years. I started as a hypnotherapist in 2003, and she was born in 2013. Sienna has been very fortunate because of those first ten years I had as a therapist. What I learned during those years came directly from my clients, many of whom were executive men years or even decades older than me and further along in life. Some already had a wife and kids. Some were men in their 40s, 50s, or 60s, while I was just a young buck in my late 20s and early 30s. What I found most interesting were the root causes of the problems my clients were experiencing.

I learned some very powerful approaches and techniques from Neuro-Linguistic Programming (NLP) in my early years of study. But I wasn't classically trained in therapy or psychology, so much of what I acquired was picked up on the job. I learned by talking to my clients about their struggles and through a particular way of asking questions that the founders of NLP developed called the meta-model. The meta-model teaches the therapist to ask very specific questions to get more and more detailed information from the individual. Using the meta-model, I often found that my clients' problems led back to similar root causes, which were experiences they had in childhood, most often related to their experiences and relationships with their parents. The pattern I saw was that experiences leading to tremendous pain, depression, anxiety, bad relationship choices, or addiction were often due to parental abuse, abandonment, and neglect. Whether it was physical, psychological, or verbal abuse wasn't as important as the fact that it taught them they weren't worthy of love.

Sometimes, it was outright neglect, like parents who didn't have the time or inclination to pay much attention to their children. Believe it or not, some parents just don't want to be parents. Then there were stories of true abandonment, where the father left before the child was born, or the mother left before the child could speak, meaning they would never see or have a relationship with their father. Or, at some point in their childhood, the parents would divorce, and either the father or the mother would soon be completely out of the picture. I heard many of these stories, specifically from people who had the most serious kinds of problems: depression, severe anxiety, people going through their second or third divorce, and people who struggled greatly in their lives. I saw these patterns emerge.

Over time, I discovered the profound significance of parenting. I developed a strong appreciation for my own family experience growing up, which I used to take for granted. When you're a child, what you're experiencing with your parents is just normal for you. Having my dad coach my baseball team, spend time with me, and say, "I love you" every night before bed was just normal for me. If we ever did get a spanking, we'd get a hug and he'd say, "You know I love you" shortly afterward. I grew up thinking that was normal. So I took my parents for granted and was mostly annoyed, whether it was by my dad's temper, sometimes his tone of voice, or his desire to control things, and I just didn't really appreciate how good I had it. And it's not just me... that's how our human brains work.

When I heard my clients' struggles and childhood experiences of abuse, neglect, and abandonment, I developed an appreciation for what I had as a child. I began to understand the kind of parent I wanted to be when I became a father. It was through those first ten years of hearing story after story that I came to understand the potential pitfalls of being a successful father. There was one client I'll never forget—a man in his 60s whose children were fully grown and had families of their own. This man had spent the better part of his kids' youth working long hours—60 or 70 hours a week—creating wealth and providing abundantly for his family in a material sense, putting his kids through school and all those things. During the course of a session, he said the exact words I've come to hear from many others since: "I wish I spent more time with my kids." He was quite sad, and it was at a point in his life where he really couldn't do anything about it. Because, as we all know, you can't go back in time.

He was one of many who learned that lesson too late. As a therapist, I'm immensely grateful for the ability to learn from others' mistakes. When I have seen clients expressing tremendous regret, sorrow, or pain about something they've gone through in their lives, it's left an impression on me. I've made a strong point of avoiding those mistakes. I can still remember that client's face. At that moment, I made a deep decision that I would spend a lot of time with my kids when I became a parent.

PRIORITIZING FAMILY

When Shelli and I got married and talked about having kids, I was already planning for the balanced life I was going to live. Now, you have to think about this from my perspective. By 2013, I had an established practice that had been thriving for several years. I always had a waiting list. I always had clients calling me. I always had more business than I could handle, meaning that if I wanted to work seven days a week and make more money, I could have done that. But I chose not to. I decided not to do that for not only my own mental and physical well-being but also because I wanted to spend time with my kid.

I've worked only four days a week since my daughter was born. During those early years, I was home. When she was an infant, a toddler learning to crawl, I was there, pointing a camera in her face. The first time she crawled, I got it on video. Her first steps, when she went from letting go of the little walker to taking her first steps on her own, I got it all on video.

I was there with the camera, with my wife giggling in the background and my daughter giggling in the foreground as she took her first three steps without grabbing onto anything. I was there for those moments. I was changing diapers and pushing her in a stroller through the park while my wife was at work. Some men think that's not masculine. I disagree. I was there with my daughter, tickling her and making her giggle, playing with her, rocking her to sleep, feeding her bottles, putting her down for nap time, taking her to the park, and all those activities that are typically handled by moms. The stereotypical male executive spends all his time going to work and bringing home the bacon. But I figured out a way to do both. I figured out how to be at home as much as possible while also running a thriving practice, serving clients, and doing something I loved. I was able to be a part-time stay-at-home dad while running a full-time practice and performing 1,000 sessions a year.

When I was at work, I worked hard. I conducted 20–30 sessions a week between 2010 and 2020, when I began to reduce my workload. But I was doing what some people say you can't do—bringing in a multiple six-figure income while also being there for my kid, helping out at home, and consistently going to the gym. During those early years of my daughter's life, I played pickup basketball at the gym two or three times a week. Later, I attended Krav Maga classes twice a week. I've done kickboxing, swimming, running, and weightlifting. I've never let up.

Those are the things I've been able to do, and I've done them because I've learned things that some men have never learned. Not everyone gets to be a therapist; not everyone gets to listen to stories from people who are decades further along in life. I'm here to share that information with you so you can change your direction. If you're putting 80% or more of your energy into your career and leaving crumbs for your health, your kids, or your marriage, you need to wake up. This is your red alert. This is the time to begin doing things differently, to learn from the mistakes of others so that someday you can have what I have—a great connection with my child and the knowledge that she has the foundation and confidence to have great relationships and thrive in whatever direction she wants to go in life.

That's ultimately what this is about. It's about redefining what legacy means. It's not just leaving a big pile of money for your kids to spend when you're gone. It's about giving them knowledge, love, and confidence, along with your heart and soul, so they'll be empowered to thrive independently. When empowered, they can make their own money and find healthy relationships. When you take care of yourself, you become a role model who shows them that it's important to take care of their own health, go to the gym, eat healthy, and spend time with their loved ones.

So this is my warning to you: That's what this book is all about. Listen to these words. Learn from the mistakes of the men whose stories I share in these pages, and begin to integrate some of these ideas into your own life. Up until now, there has been no playbook for Executive Dads. There has been no set of rules or instructions that tell you what it makes sense to do when you have the ability to earn a ton of income. Whether you're earning six figures, multiple six figures, seven figures, or running an eight- or nine-figure company, it doesn't really matter. The dilemma you have is yours. You must decide how to use your time and your energy. If you go down the familiar path, the role of the Executive Dad has been that of the provider. That makes a lot of sense, given the struggles that humanity has had to overcome. Up until very recently in human history, the father had to be the provider because the mother had to take care of the children. The father, being physically stronger, had to perform labor that required more physical strength. It was by necessity that the man would be the provider.

Men and women have just been trying to survive. Men never had the time or luxury to invest more in taking care of children, being there for their families, and being a greater presence at home. So, dads have not been expected to be caregivers. The traditional role was a man going to work, coming home, and, like Ward Cleaver, reading a newspaper in front of the fireplace. The woman took care of the children, cleaned the house, and kept everything in order. But that role in our society is rapidly evolving, partly due to technology.

REDEFINING WORK

We no longer need to work as long as we used to just to survive. Remember, that's how life used to be. We worked in the fields, on a farm, or in a factory. It used to be intensive physical labor that was required just to get enough food and provide shelter and clothing to survive. And that's only changed very recently in human history. As our reality, technology, and society change and evolve, our expectations are changing. If you have enough money to live an abundant life, then naturally, the bills are paid, and your family's needs are met. If that's the case, working 60, 70, or 80 hours a week is not a necessity. It's a choice.

Before you shake your head and start to tell me, "No, I have to work that many hours. I have to do this, I have to do that," I've heard these stories from other men before. The truth is that you're in control of your life. If you're an executive, whether you're the CEO of a multimillion-dollar company or an entrepreneur running a small business, you're in control of your time. All of us are in control of our time. We all get to decide how much of our time we invest in one thing or another: how much time we invest in work, how much time we invest in play, how much time we invest in physical exercise or health, how much time we spend with our families. You're in control of that. That means that if you've chosen to work 60 to 80 hours a week in a way that negatively impacts your health and causes your relationships to decline, that's a choice that needs to be reevaluated. You know at your core that you don't need to do that in order for your family to survive. You may feel a need to do that in order to maintain your quality of life, but it's not about survival. You may have a desire to prove something to yourself or others, but it's still not about survival. You might say, "Well, you can never have enough saved up for a rainy day." But if you go by that metric, it doesn't make sense to ever take a day off, take a vacation, or spend a single second with your loved ones. Hell, why even bother sleeping? Go make more money to add to the pile! There could be another pandemic! A zombie apocalypse! Another Civil War!

True, there is no telling what the future will bring. But there has to be some balance. If you allowed fear to completely run your life, you'd never get into a car because fatal accidents happen every day. You'd never enter a relationship because you could get your heart broken. But you know that's no way to live. And if you're an executive or entrepreneur, you're no coward. You're not content settling for a "normal life." You take calculated risks. You strive for something better. You're courageous. You want it *all*.

Any parent knows this: Young children would rather have your time and attention than your money. That means if your pursuit of additional wealth (beyond survival) is preventing you from spending enough time with your children, then you're doing it wrong. You could forgive yourself for making that mistake if you didn't know any better or if you didn't even think about it that way until now. But once you realize it, once you have that moment, once you have that epiphany, the cat's out of the bag, the genie's out of the bottle, and you can't stuff them back in. Your wife and children also know intuitively that you don't need to be working that much. They ultimately see that it's a choice, and that's what's so important about this. It's different for the blue-collar dad working two jobs just to keep the lights on.

In that reality, his kids know he has to go to work. His wife knows that he has to go to work. They know he'd rather be home, but he's doing it just to keep the lights on. But it's different when you're an executive earning a six- or seven-figure salary. It's different when you have all the "stuff" because they intuitively know that what you're doing is a choice. I know this because many clients of mine—adult children of successful men—have told me so in their own words. Your children, at some point, realize that you're choosing to work instead of being with them. That's something that we're going to talk about in more detail later.

26

SETTING EXPECTATIONS

The problem you have in creating balance in your life is related to the expectations you've set for yourself because those expectations are no longer in sync with your true reality in the present. One quick example of a similar phenomenon is that, until very recently in human history, food has been scarce. So, it's not a surprise that one of the greatest struggles we have in America in the 21st century is fighting obesity. For the first time in human history, we have an abundance of food. Our bodies have not yet adapted to that reality. When we eat sugars, fats, and salts, our bodies give us these wonderful feelings that say, "Yes! Have more of this!" All the way up until very recently, that would have been a helpful signal. Your body would want you to consume more calories so you could gain excess fat that would burn off during the lean times. But our bodies haven't yet evolved to understand that famine is no longer a thing, at least not for many of us.

One example of a person whose programming was outdated is a client that I saw not too long ago. This client grew up in Italy in a very poor environment. When he was a young boy, his family barely met their basic needs, including with respect to food. His father, uncles, and the men in his community looked at any man who wasn't working with disdain. Life was so harsh in their reality that a man who was sitting around and not working was viewed as a loser. In that community at that time, that was a legitimate criticism. In that community, when there was a level of poverty if a man wasn't working to feed and support his family, he was a loser because he had no right to be sitting idly. He had no right to waste time at home when his family needed him to provide.

My client lived for many years in this environment and formed strong opinions and beliefs about what it meant to be a man during those years. He would have been around his father, uncles, relatives, and other men in his community, and he would have heard his father talk about this not just once or twice but repeatedly over the years with great emotion and intensity. Poverty places so much pressure and stress on people that it hardwired those kinds of beliefs into my client in a very powerful way. One thing I've learned is that beliefs are based on repetition and authority. My client struggled with this on a deep level because the old way of doing things he had learned in Italy as a kid was causing problems in his current reality in America. His marriage was struggling, and he rarely spent time with his young son.

The reason for this was that he had four or five different businesses spread across two states that were consuming his time and attention. When you run four or five different businesses, the work never really ends. If you're reading this book and you're a business owner or an executive, you realize that the bigger your businesses grow and the more you take on, there's always more to do. You're never really done. It's not like working a nine-to-five job where you go home and watch the football game. It never ends. There's always something to think about. There are always new problems to solve. There's always more to do.

The problem with this client was that his values and beliefs were telling him that the right thing to do was to always be working. When he was working, he felt really good. He felt good about himself when he was creating wealth. He felt productive. He felt validated. But when he was home, spending time with his wife and son, he always felt pressure to check his phone for messages, return that phone call, send that text message, put out that fire, and help out the manager or employee. He felt this constant pressure to continue working and creating value. The problem is that he had more money than he really needed and a better quality of life than the men back in Italy in his youth could ever dream of having. The truth is that he didn't need to work that hard. He didn't need to run all those businesses. He didn't need to put that many hours or that much of his time into it for his family to not only be safe but to thrive.

His child wasn't old enough to get it yet, but his wife certainly understood that this was a choice on his part. She was becoming increasingly unhappy with the lack of time and attention from him when he was at home. She knew that if he backed off work a little bit, they would still be financially secure. But he struggled profoundly with even the concept of easing off the gas pedal, of just slowing things down a little bit and learning to work more efficiently. Throughout our sessions, I helped him be more focused on his family while at home and less distracted by work. I helped him get comfortable putting his phone on silent so he could just spend time with his kid and give him his undivided attention. During our sessions, he began to work less and spend more time at home. He helped out more around the house and had more quality interactions with his wife. But he needed his values and priorities to shift. We're talking about a couple of decades of programming that said, "Not working means that you're a loser," along with the irrational fear that, "If you slow down, your competitors will overtake you, and you'll lose everything." No matter how much wealth we accumulate, no matter how much we accomplish or do, we can always imagine losing everything. One way I was able to help him was by teaching him to control and discipline his mind and thoughts—to eliminate the irrational fear—so he could be a better husband and father.

We have to evolve. We Executive Dads have a responsibility to evolve in a way that reflects our current reality. We're no longer simply trying to survive. If developing greater balance in your life will create a better relationship with your kids, helping them grow and mature in a better way, and that balance will also result in you having a higher quality of life, better health, and a longer life, then it makes sense to evolve. Otherwise, you'll have lots of money but very little else of value. When your health is in bad shape and your relationships suck, it's very hard to be happy. I believe that happiness is a noble pursuit. To balance those things out, some of that energy needs to be withdrawn from work.

We're going to talk more in the pages to come about exactly how to make that happen. I know that at this moment, it may feel scary. It may even give you some anxiety. Hell, it may even make you want to put down the book and stop reading. But I strongly encourage you to continue. Because I know something you don't, which is that there are changes you can make in the way you think, feel, and behave that will balance out your life and give your children the father they deserve, your wife the husband she deserves, and you the life that you deserve.

CHAPTER 3
WHERE IT LEADS FOR DAD, THE MARRIAGE, AND THE KIDS

As you're beginning to understand, balancing those important areas of life is incredibly important for the Executive Dad. But I want to talk about where it leads if your life remains unbalanced. The number one reason that CEO marriages fail is lack of time for family.[1]

I'm going to speak directly from specific conversations I've had with clients who were Executive Dads. These men usually come to see me when they're at a breaking point and starting to notice the consequences of their unbalanced lives. As a therapist, I have a tremendous amount of compassion for all of my clients, and I have a special compassion for these Executive Dads who are struggling. I want to make it perfectly clear that I don't believe any of them consciously realize they're making these mistakes. I don't think they're evil or stupid. They just don't understand the true nature of

---

1. Eliott C. McLaughlin, "The CEO and Marriage: How Do the Most Successful Couples Make It Work?" *CNN*, September 30, 2018, https://www.cnn.com/2018/09/30/success/ceo-marriage/index.html.

their struggles. They contact me for help when they're experiencing pain. I'm going to share with you some important stories of clients who sought my assistance, where they were, what they were struggling with, and how it's related to the structure of their lives and their priorities.

The first client that comes to mind is an attorney who came to me on the verge of divorce. His wife had already threatened divorce and indicated that she wanted a separation. He was a mess. He was feeling very insecure about losing her. He was having her followed because he wanted to know where she was going during the day. He was tasked with watching their small children during the day while his wife, who may have been experiencing a midlife crisis, was away for extended periods. His life was quickly devolving into chaos. He had been working 60 to 80 hours a week for about a decade. During those years, he worked very hard and put in all that effort because he saw it as his primary responsibility to provide for his family.

To him, providing for his family meant working as hard as he could and generating as much wealth as he could. Like many of the clients I've seen over the years, his childhood experiences with his parents set him up for this dynamic. The pressure he put on himself to perform at such a high level was related to his own childhood experiences. Parents often motivate their children to succeed professionally because they want them to be safe and secure. But the way that message is delivered can create an imbalance, making kids conclude that their value is directly related to their productivity. So if they're not producing, they feel as if they have no value.

My client was working very hard because he genuinely believed that was his role and the right thing to do. But while he was working so much, there was not much time left for his marriage or even managing his health. He was buried in his office, working all hours, barely coming up for air. His wife wasn't receiving what she needed from her husband. When you don't have time to talk to your partner, to bond with them, to do things with them, to go on a date night, to have downtime together, eventually you drift apart. And that's what happened with his marriage. By the time he came to see me, it was too late.

The situation with his wife became worse and more chaotic. I supported him in maintaining his composure and a positive mindset while helping him understand how he got into this situation and the root of the problems he was experiencing with his wife. Here's a man who is desperately trying to take care of his small children while trying to understand his wife's erratic behavior after working more than a decade to provide wealth and a great quality of life. He'd fulfilled the role he thought was his to fill—being a provider. The chaos and pain he suffered through, as it became apparent that his wife not only desired a divorce but had already begun an affair with another man, was awful. Watching him deal with the repercussions of his past choices was a sad sight, to say the least. I see it as my job to both guide clients through difficult waters and help them understand the root cause of their pain. If you blame someone or something outside yourself for your problems, then logically, it would take someone or something outside yourself to fix it. We have to own our lives as well as our mistakes in order to move forward independently.

But nothing absolves the wife of responsibility for her own actions. I've worked many hundreds of hours with husbands and wives dealing with the difficulties of marriage. I've worked with cheaters and the "cheatees," helping them learn from their mistakes and make better decisions moving forward. It should go without saying that the right thing to do in this situation is to communicate with your spouse and find a better alternative than marital infidelity. She's responsible for her choices. But actions have consequences. What I want you to focus on is your ability to control yourself and your actions. Make no excuses. No one but you is going to change your life. That's on you. That's the message I embed in the unconscious minds of clients like this one. Following our sessions, and after my client has gone through his divorce, he'll be able to create a more balanced life with healthy relationships that allow him to succeed in all areas—not just his career.

Another client in a similar position was a CEO who came to see me in a desperate state. His wife was similarly threatening divorce. He believed that if he just pulled it together and started to change his behavior, he could save the marriage. I took him on as a client with the clear understanding that I couldn't promise him that working with me would save his marriage. That depended in large part upon his wife and what she wanted as well. But I told him that regardless of how things went, I would help him handle whatever happened as well as possible. As we began our sessions, he came to reveal what he discovered was the root cause of his marital problem: He'd been doing so well as a CEO that when he was at home, he wasn't contributing. He was usually very tired from working and very worn out. He admittedly was unaware or at least had not given much attention to his wife's expectations for him at home.

That meant simple things like the upkeep of the house, helping out with their young child, and other things that most women in this day and age are expecting from their husbands, regardless of how much money they make. He even confessed to being lazy and passive around the house. The energy his wife observed in him was that of someone who wasn't contributing. She felt overwhelmed with taking care of all the responsibilities in the household while he seemed to only go to work and come home, and that's it. He admitted to making a big mistake and contributing to his wife's dissatisfaction. On one occasion, I met with his wife to assess whether she felt the marriage could be saved, and her response was crystal clear: she was 100% already out the door. She was angry. She was over it. She had no passion left in her heart. She had love for him as a person, but the marriage had deteriorated for so long that it was no longer salvageable in her view. Our sessions focused on helping him become a better man while navigating the unfortunate separation.

PREVENTING HEARTBREAK

The more men I encountered at this late stage of the game, the more it occurred to me that I wanted to help them at an earlier stage. That's why I'm writing this book. Because when you get to the point where your wife is already on the verge of divorce, where the marriage has deteriorated to such an extent that it's no longer salvageable, it's too late in the game. There's a lot of pain that follows, which may be off your radar, that you might not be expecting, and that you might have no awareness of at all. I want to talk in more detail about that because there are significant costs for the Executive Dad who takes his eye off the ball.

There are costs for placing all your eggs in one basket (work, career, and quality of life), which you'd never do with your investments. There is excessive stress, anxiety, and ultimately depression. These are symptoms of an unbalanced life, often related to self-perception. The way you organize your life is a reflection of your self-perception, your identity, what you think your role is, and what you think your responsibilities are. One of the things that often gets overlooked is, well—what's in it for you? How important are your needs? How important is it to have time to relax, to see your friends, to have fun with your wife and kids? When these things are overlooked, it's often a symptom of a man who doesn't quite value himself or his own happiness, his own sense of fulfillment. I find this to be pervasive. The relentless fixation on work, business, and money leads to excessive anxiety and stress. Because no matter how much money you make or how successful your business is, there is always more to worry about. To repeat, when you're a CEO or an entrepreneur, the list of things to do never ends.

You're in charge of when you start working and when you stop. It's very different from the traditional role of showing up for a job, clocking in at 9 o'clock, and clocking out at 5 o'clock. You go home and spend time with your family or loved ones. You go to the ball-game at night with your friends. When you're an executive or entrepreneur, you're always tempted to work. Because the thoughts about problems that need to be solved, the thoughts about things that need to be done, the endless list of to-dos, the employees to manage, the planning that needs to be done, the meetings to arrange —the list never ends. The problem with this is that if there is no point at which you can tell yourself that it's okay to slow down, it's okay to take the afternoon off, it's okay to spend some time with your kids, it's okay to do something with your wife, then that never-ending cycle creates a powerful feeling of anxiety and stress. It's not objective reality that determines your emotional state. It's what you're thinking about and focusing on. Therefore, if you're always thinking about problems, if you're always thinking about work, if you're always thinking about that next thing that needs to be done, you're going to be in a state of heightened stress and tension. It makes no difference whether you have $10 million or $10 in the bank. It's a product of your thoughts, your thinking, and your focus.

It used to surprise me when I heard stories from men who were multimillionaires but anxious all the time. When I was young, unem-ployed, and broke (which is who I was and how I was when I first began my hypnotherapy practice), I would hear these stories and think, *Wow, I always thought if I just had $10,000 in the bank, I'd have no worries at all.* I came to find that men could be very, very worried even with $10 million in the bank. That's because it's all about how we think.

Another client of mine was a perfect example of this. He came to me in a desperate state. His business was really booming, and he was stuck in a cycle where the stress would become overwhelming every couple of weeks. From everything he described to me, he was generating millions of dollars per year in revenue, and it was increasing exponentially to the point where he was always busy. He never wasn't checking his phone. He was going on fantastic voyages and trips, rubbing elbows with billionaires. He never got a break because of all this growth and the time it required. Because of that, it created a cycle where, every couple of weeks, he would go on a bender and engage in all sorts of risky behavior as a means of releasing tension and stress because that was his only outlet. This pattern was beginning to cost him.

He had children who were being affected by his behavior. At times, they saw him in a bad state—either extremely stressed and frenetic or perhaps under the influence. When I spoke with him, he was absolutely sincere and completely desperate in his desire to fix his behavior, create a change, and get his life in order. Not only was this causing damage in his marriage, his children, and his health, but it was also something that could completely blow up and destroy his career, which had become his absolute obsession. If he got into any legal trouble, it could severely damage his most important business relationships or perhaps even sever them completely. The good news is that once we began working together, he was able to organize his thoughts and his mind in such a way that reduced the stress and anxiety. He was starting to mend the situation with his marriage and his children. But his situation had reached a breaking point where he was putting his health, his marriage, and his relationship with his children at risk due to the unbalanced life he'd created.

While those are very clear and significant problems, these are well-intentioned men who were trying to do the right thing. They were trying to be responsible. They were trying to be successful. They wanted to create wealth and security for their wives and children. On a deeper level, all of them had expressed a desire to create some sort of a legacy for their children or even their grandchildren.

They aspired to create enough wealth so their children, grandchildren, and great-grandchildren would never have to worry about money again. This unbalanced life comes from good intentions. It comes from an honest intention of wanting to be a good man, wanting to do the right thing, and wanting to create safety and security for your loved ones. But it's not well thought out, and these are the problems it causes. You know what they say about good intentions. The result is problems with your physical and emotional health, problems with your relationships and marriage, and ultimately self-destruction. That could also destroy your career and all the wealth you've created.

Most successful men are aware of the significant cost of divorce. Allowing the marriage to deteriorate not only results in the deterioration of a relationship, which can be devastating personally and emotionally, but it can also cause anxiety, stress, and depression for both parties in the marriage, as well as significant damage to the children. It can also disrupt and destroy your career. It can ruin your bank account and eat away at all the assets you worked so hard to achieve. It can cause you to be less productive and less focused on important decisions you need to make for your business. This means your life must be balanced in order to avoid watching it spiral out of control.

If you, as the Executive Dad, don't make a priority of balancing your life and creating enough time for your relationships, your marriage, your children, and your health, it could lead to the dissolution of your most cherished relationships, separation and divorce, heartache, and pain. It could lead to distant relationships with your children over time. It could lead to addictions to alcohol, drugs, food, and more. It leads to stress, behavior swings, regret, and fatigue. It can lead to infidelity. It can lead to your marriage deteriorating to the point where you just don't have intimacy, and you don't feel love, and men who aren't getting that type of fulfillment from their relationship are much more prone to seek it outside of it. The same goes for your wife because the wife of a man who's not giving her any time or attention is more likely to seek that fulfillment outside of the marriage. All of those behaviors cause even more guilt and regret.

Ultimately, an unhealthy marriage—one that isn't filled with love, in which the father and the mother are distant and don't express affection—negatively impacts the children's ability to form a healthy relationship of their own when the time comes. I'm telling you this as a therapist who's heard many stories from the children of successful dads who were never around and didn't spend much time with them. I've heard the stories of children whose parents had a loveless marriage and how that made it very difficult for them to know what a healthy relationship even looked like. The symptoms and consequences of an unbalanced life, when you realize just how bad it can get, really give you powerful motivation to rethink the way you're organizing your life. Remember, you're the CEO of "You, Inc." You're in control of your time. You make all the important decisions about how you run your life. No matter how difficult it may appear, it's absolutely possible to reorganize, restructure, and change your life. You can take control of your life. You can do things in a better way.

To conclude this chapter, I'd like you to answer a few questions.

1. How many hours per week are you devoting to work?
2. How many hours per week are you devoting to your marriage? Specifically, how many hours are you setting aside just to spend quality time with your wife?
3. How many hours are you specifically allocating for your child(ren)? I'm referring to time devoted to hanging out with them, spending time with them, doing things with them, and giving them your full attention.

4. How many hours per week are you devoting to physical activity and exercise? For many Executive Dads I meet, work receives 90% or more of their attention. What's left over for their relationships and health are just the scraps. So, do the math and ask yourself: *Is the amount of time I'm devoting to work versus the amount of time that I'm devoting to my relationships and health an honest expression of my priorities?*

5. Is this what you want for your child(ren)? Ask yourself: *Is the life I'm living now the kind of life I'd want my own kids to live one day? Would I want them to work as much as I do? Would I want them to be in the state of health that I'm in now?* It's something to think about.

CHAPTER 4
SUCCESSFUL DADS OR PARENTS OF SUCCESSFUL DADS

One thing I find to be completely off the radar for most Executive Dads is the challenges their children will face. In my years as a hypnotherapist, I've worked with a great number of clients who came from successful parents and grew up living abundant lives. They had plenty of money, went to great schools, had good friends, and all the things anyone could ever desire. But they had unique challenges related to growing up in that kind of environment. I'm talking about children as young as eight years old all the way up to adults in their 20s, 30s, and 40s, whose lives have been impacted by their childhood experiences and their relationships with their Executive Dads.

One story that often comes to mind is of a young female client I saw several years ago who had a very successful father. Her story about her father reminded me of one of my favorite movies of all time, *Ferris Bueller's Day Off*. Her father had this Aston Martin that he absolutely loved. He spent a lot of time polishing it, looking at it, and taking it out for Sunday drives. But from my client's perspective, her dad absolutely hated everyone in his family. He frequently yelled at his wife and daughter. Most of the interaction she had with him was combative. They would go on elaborate vacations to beautiful destinations but wouldn't talk to each other. They'd all be looking at their phones. They were distracted, and there wasn't much love or genuine human connection.

As this young woman told her story, I recalled Ferris Bueller's friend Cameron and how they "borrowed" his dad's Ferrari. Watching as an adult with experience as a therapist, I found it amusing that the license plate on his dad's Ferrari read *"NRVOUS."* When I saw that movie as a kid, I had no idea the significance of the dad having a license plate that said "nervous." But given what I now know about wealthy men, it made a lot of sense. I strongly believe that director John Hughes had very close contact at some point in his life with men like Cameron's dad—men of wealth, men of abundant success, Executive Dads—because that license plate would be a perfect description of so many men of wealth who never stop thinking about work, who pride themselves on their accomplishments, and buy the Ferrari (or the Aston Martin) either to show others how successful they've been or in an attempt to find happiness through material consumption. And I say this as a man who loves sports cars. There was a time when I wanted one badly. At this point in my life, I have other priorities.

I found that insecurity is a big part of what drives many men (and women) to become wildly successful. They need to prove something to themselves, their families, their spouses, and their high school friends. They feel like they have something to prove because they don't really feel all that great about themselves emotionally. So, that NRVOUS license plate really makes a lot of sense. It's a very accurate description of the man Cameron and Ferris described, who had a house like a museum where you couldn't touch anything and had a very negative relationship with his wife and son. As I sat talking to my young client about her father and her relationship with him, how unhealthy it was, and how angry he seemed to be, I found it to be tremendously sad. Here was a man who clearly had worked very, very hard. He wasn't lazy, but he had made a mistake when setting his priorities. He apparently hadn't made a point of establishing a strong connection and relationship with his daughter. As a father of a young girl, I find that to be incredibly sad. At the time of this writing, my daughter and I have an incredibly solid relationship. She confides in me. We laugh and play games together. We have serious talks about life and all sorts of things.

Because of that, I'm optimistic that when she's a young woman, we'll still be very, very close. The relationship changes as the child grows older, but if you make it a priority, the connection can become even stronger. This client's dad had clearly dropped the ball. She described him as an angry man, which doesn't make any sense to the average blue-collar person. Here's a multimillionaire with an Aston Martin, taking elaborate vacations to faraway places and yelling at his wife and daughter all the time. But in my experience as a hypnotherapist, it actually does make some sense because what he's doing in his head is what's creating that anger and volatility.

The result of his choices is what has eroded his relationships with his wife and daughter. (This is not to say that the man is 100% responsible for every argument with his family; instead, the pattern is a sign that his family relationships are out of alignment.) Because he chose to spend so much time working and more time with his car than with his child, there was an inevitable resentment that boiled in those relationships. This resentment would come out when they happened to spend time together, typically while on vacation. Sadly, they couldn't even enjoy those vacations because of how angry they were with each other, because of the things they never said to each other, or because of problems that evolved in ways that remained a mystery to all the people involved.

THE COST OF DAD'S ABSENCE

Remember, children of wealthy dads have different expectations. I had a client recently who didn't see her dad much when she was growing up, but she understood it was because he worked two jobs. He worked two jobs just to keep the lights on because he wasn't making much money at either job. While she missed out on having more time with him and wasn't happy about that, she didn't blame him because she knew it wasn't a choice. Children of dads who have abundant wealth but rarely spend time with them intuitively know that he's making a choice, that he's choosing not to spend time with them. He's choosing to work, play golf, or polish the Aston Martin instead. That inevitably causes those kids to question their own value. The client I'm mentioning was experiencing that same problem: insecurity. She had problems with self-esteem, depression, and anxiety. When your own father chooses to work over spending time with you, the ultimate message you conclude is that it's because there's something wrong with you. Clearly, Dad has more important things to do than spend time with you. That's how kids interpret it.

Then, because they realize he would rather do these other things than spend time with them, kids begin to wonder why. They might see friends of theirs, other kids whose fathers are around more often, and ask themselves, "What's wrong with me?" It's not something they're conscious of at the time, but when I ask my clients about it during a session, it resonates with them. At some point, they do start to wonder "why." *Why doesn't my dad want to spend more time with me? Why is he working so much? Why is he never there? Why doesn't he take me out like my friend's dad does? Why doesn't he have conversations with me? Why doesn't he show interest in me?* When they ask those questions, they find answers. Why? Because you can find whatever it is that you're looking for.

The questions they ask are related to their self-perception. They start wondering, *What's wrong with me? Am I not pretty enough? Am I not talented enough?* Ultimately, they wonder, *What if I'm not good enough? What if I'm not interesting enough? What if I'm not talented enough? What if I'm not beautiful enough?* It creates anxiety and depression because it influences their expectations about how other people will respond to them, whether friends, an employer, or a relationship partner. People tend to fixate on what they perceive to be their flaws.

The logic is this: If they could just identify the flaws and fix them, then maybe Dad would spend more time with them. Perhaps they would have a more positive expectation about how other people will view them, feel about them, or respond to them. So here's what you need to remember as an Executive Dad: Choosing to consistently prioritize work over your children ultimately leads to your children questioning their value, resulting in depression and anxiety, while they harbor resentment toward you for making that choice. They conclude that they're not worth Dad's time.

"But that's not all!" as they used to say in late-night infomercials. There are other challenges that the children of successful dads experience, one of which is being spoiled. It's easy for wealthy men to give their children money because it doesn't require much time. Instead of giving their children time (which is limited and thus more valuable), many wealthy men give their kids money. Some of them think that's a good thing that will make their kids happy.

They buy them toys. They take them on fancy vacations. They buy them cars, electronics, games, and all the "stuff" that kids could ever want. However, when kids receive too much "stuff" when they're young, it creates a huge problem as they grow older. They become spoiled. The way the brain works is that it filters out what's normal. When you receive all this stuff—if you are always eating at nice restaurants and staying at fancy resorts—it just becomes... normal. It gets filtered out. That's what "spoiled" means. It means these children who grew up with abundant wealth and whose dads have given them all this "stuff" are very difficult to impress. After all, when you grow up with abundant wealth, what can you do that's more impressive than what you've already experienced throughout your entire childhood?

It also saps the child's enthusiasm to go out there as an adult and create their own way in life. Because if you already have financial security, then what's the point of working hard? I've seen that in many young adults. I've had many clients in their 20s and 30s who grew up with such wealth that they never really tried hard to create their own career or business, to go out there and make it on their own, because they were already too comfortable. Their parents allowed them to stay at home well into their 20s and 30s and let them live off their wealth. It saps their motivation to go out and do their own thing. The problem with that should be obvious to the high-achieving dad!

On an emotional level, there's something incredibly satisfying about making your own way in life, about starting with nothing as I did and creating a life that's better than you ever thought it could be. For children with wealthy parents, if they're given everything but time from their father and mother, the challenge is that nothing for the rest of their lives will really impress them. No amount of wealth or abundance will ever fulfill them. They will also have very little sense of purpose and no real feeling of accomplishment. Money also provides easy access to things that can cause kids trouble, like drugs, alcohol, the "wrong crowd," etc. Those are just some of the challenges your kids will face.

Children are naturally predisposed to curiosity, to looking into things, to wanting to find out, to having experiences, to testing boundaries. When parents give them lots and lots of wealth and don't give them lots and lots of time, that sometimes leads to kids finding out the hard way. Whether that's with drugs, alcohol, sex, relationships, or risky behavior—the propensity for those types of experiences is amplified in a family that has become wealthy. I've seen these adults who essentially feel eternally adolescent, like their bodies are older, but they still feel emotionally like kids because they've never really taken on any true responsibility. They don't really know what they're made of. They don't feel any sense of accomplishment. They never really felt worthy and deserving of Dad's love or respect. In terms of what they can accomplish in life, even if they work hard, it's very difficult to equal or exceed Dad's achievements. Many of us grow up in an environment where you could start poor and then become middle class or start middle class and become upper middle class or even upper class. But where is there to go when you already started at the top?

THE SUCCESS OF THE NEXT GENERATION

As you may know personally, there's something very satisfying about creating a better quality of life than the generation that came before you. But when a father becomes highly successful, it creates a new challenge for his kids. This came up in a conversation I had with a good friend who has become a very successful CEO. He has two boys who, at the time of this writing, are about to head off to college. My friend expressed concern that it will be very difficult for them to do better than he's done professionally. For his sons to be able to go out and improve upon the quality of life they had growing up would be incredibly challenging. They could do it, but it would just be very difficult. We naturally compare ourselves to our parents and others who came before us.

It doesn't mean his sons can't be successful or happy if their father is incredibly successful. It just means that it's an additional challenge. It's something of which the Executive Dad needs to be aware. If you're a successful man creating this kind of wealth and you have children, then you really need to devote time and energy to preparing them mentally and emotionally for the challenges ahead. You'll need to help them understand something I believe to be fundamentally true. It's extremely important that my own child knows this and, in fact, that everyone in the world knows this: Your value is not related to how much money you earn. Your value is not contingent on your job title or your accomplishments. I believe that our human value is intrinsic. That means we're born with it. What you go out and achieve and accomplish is a result of your actions. It's a reflection of how hard you've worked, what you've learned, and your ability to take advantage of the opportunities you've had. But it's not your value. It's not even your identity. I want my friend's boys to know that they don't have to achieve more than their dad does to feel successful in life or feel good about themselves.

If you're not having that conversation with your kids because you're too busy making millions of dollars, you could be setting them up for an unfortunate reality for the rest of their lives in which they feel like they haven't really accomplished much. This dynamic is actually very well represented in the popular HBO series *Succession*. The first episode immediately hooked me because I saw absolute truth in it. There you have Brian Cox as the father who has created this empire, a multi-billion-dollar conglomerate and media enterprise. The entire series is about his adult children vying for the opportunity to succeed him as the CEO and leader of the empire as he grows older and begins having serious health problems. What you see as the series develops is just how unhappy, unfulfilled, and emotionally unstable the children are, how terrible their relationships are, and how difficult it is for them to feel good about themselves—

all because they've desperately spent their entire lives seeking their dad's approval.

Watching the opening titles of the show, you see a dad who was either physically or mentally absent from his kids. His adult children all have wild emotional swings—whether addicted to drugs, engaged in unhealthy sexual relationships, or struggling with depression and anxiety. It's all due to having a dad who gives them money or opportunity instead of giving them his time. He never really validates their worth. In fact, he measures them by their accomplishments and their potential to take over the company. So, the inherent competition to become the CEO of their father's empire is as much about winning his love and approval as it is about achieving something on their own.

The ultimate message here is that your kids don't really need your money—or at least not that much of it. What they really need is your time. What they need is your guidance. What they need is your love. Those things are so much more precious and valuable than any amount of money or wealth that you could either give them or leave to them when you're gone. Certain dynamics emerge in a family of abundant wealth. If this is either your current situation or one you're working toward, you need to know this to prevent serious traumatic experiences from occurring within your family.

The dynamic I've just touched upon—money being a substitute for time or love from yourself or your wife—is significant. Because your time is so precious, it can be tempting just to throw money at your kids and think it will keep them busy or make them happy. It's more than just giving them money to spend to have fun. I'm also talking about putting them in excellent schools, giving them all the best opportunities, and even keeping them safe by living in a very affluent neighborhood. It's about all these different things you can do that might make you feel good about yourself, knowing that your children are in good hands, have good teachers and good friends, and live in a good neighborhood. But there is no substitute for your time and your love. There's a serious dynamic I've learned about over the years from clients who come from a *Succession*-type family: Everything becomes entangled with money.

One of my clients came from a family with an empire of its own. All the children inevitably became entangled with the family business. They all worked for the business, their investments were controlled by the family, or they would not be allowed to participate in the family business. When the family business is so successful, the path to establishing their own wealth and success is so strongly associated with the family that they're in a situation that's almost impossible to navigate. All of the family events—everything from the family vacations to the family reunions—are all about the business.

Because everything is related to business and money, the severe dysfunction comes from the fact that children growing up in this environment don't really know how their family members feel about them. They don't really know whether anyone genuinely cares for them, loves them, has an agenda, or perhaps is trying to manipulate them. So, it creates confusion with respect to what's arguably most important in a family, which is trust and love. When money is associated with all these different aspects of their lives, it really becomes inextricable, and that creates mental and emotional instability. Ultimately, it leads to those classic symptoms of anxiety, stress, and depression, not to mention drug addiction, which is rampant among the wealthy.

Generational trauma is a concept that has become more and more popular of late. I'm specifically referring to the patterns that are repeated from one generation to the next within families. The trauma works like this: Children who grow up with abusive parents are programmed in such a way that makes it much more likely that they'll abuse their own children someday as well. It's what they know. The experiences we have when we're growing up influence our thought patterns. Our immediate subjective experience creates the patterns that determine our thoughts, emotions, and behaviors throughout the rest of our lives. Now, do I believe in free will? Absolutely. But that doesn't mean this pattern isn't incredibly difficult for people to overcome. When you don't receive love, it's very difficult to know how to give it. When you're abused, neglected, or harmed in some way, it becomes very easy just to repeat those same kinds of patterns. They're familiar. So this cycle continues to repeat over and over and over again, and it just gets worse and worse and worse over time. If you, as a father, are not showing your child love or not giving your child your time, what do you expect your child to be able to give to their own children someday? This is where you want to think a bit differently about legacy and start thinking about your grandchildren, your great-grandchildren, or your great-great-great-grandchildren. What you teach your child will have a huge influence on their ability to teach their own children.

So ask yourself this question: *How much love do I want my grandchildren to get from their parents?* If the answer is very little, then it makes sense to ignore your own kids, throw some money at them, and hope they'll be okay. But if you want your grandchildren to be loved, if you want your grandchildren to grow up and be emotionally stable, to have good relationships and to be healthy and happy, then you have to give that same thing to your own children, even if it means sacrificing some wealth or sacrificing some time that you normally devote to business.

I know that in my own life, my father decided that he was going to give his kids more attention than he ever got from his dad. He made an effort to be softer and less strict when disciplining us than his father was. Even though he did this imperfectly, he did it better than his dad. We knew we were loved. We had a good connection with him. He spent lots of time with us. I have taken the baton from my dad, as have my brother and sister, and none of us have ever laid a hand on our children. They're growing up well-adjusted. All of us have made significant decisions to spend lots of time with our children. My wife and I are going even further with our decision to homeschool our daughter.

The number one thing I'm doing is giving Sienna my full attention while spending time with her. It's not just that I'm taking her to lunch twice a week. It's not just that we hang out before bedtime and do things together. It's that when we're hanging out, I'm not checking my phone constantly. When I'm with her, I'm not thinking about money, work, and all the other things on my to-do list. I'm giving her my full attention. That comes from a belief that she's worthy and deserving of my attention. Also, it's good for her development, self-esteem, and self-perception. And it's good for me because I actually enjoy giving her my full time and attention. Doing so makes it more likely that we'll have the kind of conversations that make me smile or that I'll leave that interaction knowing that I did something that was good for her.

So, I prioritize spending time together with my daughter every week. It's something I create in my schedule. I have days when I go into the office, and I'm gone most of the day, and then on my off days, there is always time to spend with her. Whether it's in the morning, after she's finished with her schoolwork in the afternoon, playing a game at dinnertime, or watching a show together before she goes to bed, I prioritize spending time with her. I put it in my calendar because it's important to me. I allocate time to have meaningful conversations with her. That means when I take her to lunch on my days off, I'm not just driving to lunch and listening to music; I talk to her about meaningful things. Those meaningful conversations are an opportunity for me to download more and more of my wisdom into her brain. The more knowledge that I pass on to her, the easier it will be for her to avoid making the same mistakes I've made and live a happy and successful life.

Every night, I remind Sienna about gratitude. Yes, I literally have a reminder on my phone every night at her bedtime that says, "Remind Sienna about gratitude." So, as I say goodnight to her, I ask her, "What are you grateful for today, kiddo?" Whether it's being able to spend time with her friends, going out to lunch with dear old Dad, or going to Target with Mom, I get her to think about those things that she might otherwise take for granted. I'm creating a habit for her of focusing on things that otherwise might get filtered out. This is a way for me to prevent her from getting spoiled because, in truth, she does have more "stuff" and more opportunities than my wife or I ever did when we were her age. I am preparing her for a future of financially providing for herself. That is one of the reasons why, on multiple occasions, we've run a lemonade stand, during which we've taught her about the money that you invest in the supplies—the lemons, sugar, ice, cups—and all the things that you need to run your business. She's learning about profit margins and all that good stuff. I'm spending my time teaching my kid the fundamentals of business when I could be making more money for my family just by seeing more clients. But I'm investing that time in her so she's not dependent on me for the rest of her life and knows how to provide for herself.

I also remind Sienna that her value is intrinsic. It sounds fancy, but I explicitly explain to her that her value isn't attached to how wonderfully she plays the piano, even though she's a prodigy. Her value isn't related to how well she advances at her dance studio, even though she's doing extraordinarily well there. Her value isn't related to the grades she gets with her schoolwork or the compliments she receives from people. I teach Sienna that her value is something she's born with. I let her know repeatedly that her mother and I will love her throughout her life, no matter what she does, no matter what she does or doesn't achieve.

Those are just a few examples of what I'm doing to set my daughter up for success. I want you to ask yourself, aside from perhaps putting your kids in good schools and making sure that their needs are met, *What am I doing to set my child up for success?* As you begin to think about what else you could be doing to prepare them for happiness and independence once they've moved into adulthood, you might identify ways in which you could change and things you could be doing differently.

CHAPTER 5
EXECUTIVE DADS AND SURVIVAL BRAIN

Maybe at this point, I've got you convinced. You're reading this and thinking to yourself, *Alright, Sean. This makes sense. I recognize that this is probably a good idea. I need to start working a bit less, spending more time with my kids, making more time for my marriage, and maybe start going to the gym and taking better care of my health.* The next question you might ask yourself is, *How the hell do I do it?* This can be particularly challenging because of the phenomenon that I've come to know as the "survival brain."

One important thing to understand about your brain is that it is designed primarily to keep you alive. I'm going to talk about your brain as its own entity. When I talk about your brain and the thoughts it generates, I'm not referring to your conscious thoughts. Let me take a moment to explain what I mean.

You can identify a problem in your business or family and devote time to thinking about how to solve it. You can think about different solutions, people to consult, or resources available. You can think purposefully about where you want to go on your next vacation, whether to the beach or the mountains, and whether to invite certain friends or family members. This is thinking with intent. What I'm going to talk about next are automatic, unconscious thoughts.

The concept of the survival brain is this: When left to its own devices, your brain will focus on negative stimuli. The human brain has evolved over thousands of years, and researchers have concluded that humans have survived as a species because of our ability to anticipate and avoid danger. If you think back to the times of hunters and gatherers, if a human didn't imagine that there could be wild animals or warring tribes, they could be caught unprepared and face death. Many humans throughout history have been killed by wild animals or other humans due to their failure to be appropriately prepared for those dangers. Humans have evolved by considering various possibilities that could threaten their existence to prepare for them or prevent them from happening.

This is important to understand in the present because your brain engages in this kind of automated thinking every day. I found this fascinating when I realized my clients with tens of millions of dollars in the bank were still anxious. They're not nervous because they're not safe. Objectively, they're some of the safest humans that ever lived. Objectively, they'll never have to worry about money. They have climate control, cars, planes, and trains for travel, abundant food, and everything they need to survive. So why are they so nervous? Why are they so anxious? The answer is the survival brain. No matter how much money you have, your brain can always imagine losing it.

I've talked to clients who generate many millions of dollars every year, yet if they have a month where they make 10% less than the previous month, they start to feel nervous. And yet that "bad month" is ten times better than their best month not too long ago. This is how the survival brain evolves. It acclimates to any level of abundance or wealth. It's like the problem described in the previous chapter about spoiled kids: They eat in the best restaurants, have the nicest vacations, and it all becomes normalized, so it doesn't impress them anymore.

The problem of the survival brain means that no matter how much money you make, it's never going to make you feel safe. No amount of money or wealth will cause your brain to stop worrying. Your brain does not care about happiness. All the thoughts it generates automatically are about survival. This applies to everything from your business to your personal relationships. You might think, *What do personal relationships have to do with survival?* Well, it may not be the case now that losing a friendship means death, but in earlier times, protecting the group or community was crucial. If you didn't have the group's protection, it often led to death. While that may not be true now, your survival brain still perceives personal relationships and what people think of you as influencing your ability to navigate the world, create connections, and gain access to resources. We're social creatures. If we don't have friends, family, or people who love and care about us, life can be very lonely.

The survival brain affects how you think about every aspect of your life. Recognizing the challenge this presents is crucial. If you understand that you can't devote 90–100% of your energy and attention to your career and pursuit of wealth because of serious and undesirable consequences, the challenge becomes, *How do I retrain my brain so that I can feel comfortable doing this?* For the Executive Dads I've worked with, it can be scary to think about implementing these kinds of changes.

Even imagining backing off by 5–10% from how much they're working can cause them to fear their whole business crumbling, their fortunes dwindling, and losing those who love them. Some even believe that those who love them—whether it's their wife or their friends—are only in their lives because of their wealth. It's a terrible mental virus that, if not properly contained, can destroy your life. So what do you have to do? Number one, it starts with aligning your priorities. I've referred to three important facets of life throughout this book. I playfully call them the Trinity (I was raised Catholic) because, in many studies over the years, three aspects of life are described as being the most important.

First is **quality of life**, which refers to the home you live in, the car you drive, the restaurants you dine in, and how much money you have in the bank. If you're an Executive Dad, you have this one down pat. However, two others are equally important. One is **relationships**, and the other is **health**. If one or more of those pillars are weak, it's difficult to be happy. It's hard to be happy if you're struggling to make ends meet. It creates stress and pressure in your relationships and deprives you of the ability to enjoy certain experiences in life. It's very difficult to be happy if you don't have good relationships. If you're arguing all the time with your spouse or children, if there's no love or time for developing friendships or sharing meaningful experiences, it's difficult to be happy. It's also difficult to be happy if you're not healthy. I've had clients who have wealth and great relationships but never make time to exercise or eat healthily. They're overweight, borderline diabetic, don't sleep well, feel tired all the time, and are unhappy with their bodies. So, that pillar is also crucial. It's not just your health but also the health of your loved ones. It's tough to be happy when you have a wife or child with a chronic illness. So, if any of those three are not properly in alignment, happiness can be difficult to attain. The goal is to be as successful in all three of those areas as possible. And while you may not be able to control the health of your loved ones, you can control how you maintain your own health.

That means making serious decisions about what you devote your time to. Many men who achieve great success professionally do so by giving nearly all their time and energy to their careers and pursuit of wealth while neglecting their relationships and health. To eliminate the stress, anxiety, and resistance to balancing your life, you first need to redefine the meaning of the word "success." You might have thought of success as only about money, your house, your cars, your title, or status. But you need to redefine success as a life in which the Trinity is properly balanced—where your finances, relationships, and health are all in good shape.

As a therapist, I've come to view that as a recipe for true success. Think about it in terms of investment. A very different strategy is involved in making short-term trades versus creating a portfolio that will provide wealth for decades. Ideally, you want to be in a good situation both now and in the future. When investing your time, it's important to think about it the same way. The time you invest in your career will provide financial stability and wealth in both the short term and the long term. However, if you're not investing your time in your marriage, it will eventually unravel, resulting in serious financial, emotional, and even physical consequences—divorce, anger, stress, etc. Suppose you're not investing time in your kids. In that case, they'll eventually develop problems that will affect you in all those same ways—whether financial, as they require therapy or rehabilitation for substance abuse or other emotional issues; the emotional turmoil you suffer from watching them struggle; or physical problems related to stress caused by simply dealing with your troubled kids. If you're not investing your time in your health, that too will unravel and likely result in excessive weight gain, diabetes, ulcers, and eventually heart disease, heart attack, or stroke. Those health problems will either result in lost revenue due to an inability to work, lost time with loved ones due to a shortened life span, or both.

DEFINING SUCCESS

I'm very grateful for what I've learned from my clients because it has helped me tremendously as an individual. If I hadn't been a therapist, I, too, would likely have been guilty of living an unbalanced life. Because of what I've learned, I've redefined what success means to me. I've chosen to leave some money on the table to invest time in my child, marriage, and health. I've done that knowing that I will always have enough money. I've also redefined success in a way that detaches my sense of self-worth from the amount of money I have in the bank and what I've achieved through my career or professional life. I know the success I have with my business, the amount of money I generate, and the wealth I accrue are not evidence of my value as a human being but a product of my choices. If you choose to work hard, learn from your mistakes, and grow, then procuring a certain amount of wealth is inevitable.

If you're reading this book, you've probably learned that through experience. But when you no longer think of financial success as something you need to pursue to have value or prove your worth as a human being, it changes everything. You start to look at your life the way you might look at your business. You can't be short-sighted. You can't just put all your eggs in one basket. If you want a successful business not just this year or this quarter but for the next 10, 20, 30, 40, or even 100 years, you must be disciplined in your thinking and plan carefully.

Begin to think about your life the way you think about your business. Consider where you want to be when you're 60, 70, or 80 years old. Because when you start to think about that, it changes what you do today. If you have a goal for your business and all your thoughts are focused just on this next fiscal year, you'll make very different decisions about what to do than if you're thinking about where you want to be 10 or 20 years from now. And conversely, if you're only focused on how much money you're going to generate this coming year, you'll take a very different course of action than if you think about where you want to be in 10 or 20 years with your physical health, your relationship with your kids, and your marriage.

So once you understand that success is about more than wealth, you have to change your thinking. Success is about happiness, and happiness is only achieved when you balance **the Trinity of financial health, relationship health, and physical/mental health**. Once you discover that, it makes sense to allocate your time more carefully.

I often find that clients have accrued a massive amount of wealth because they've been on a mission since a very young age. And that mission has been well-intentioned but misaligned. Recall when I explained that when children grow up with parents who don't show them enough time or love, they might grow up doubting their own value. They think, *If my own parents didn't care about me, why should anyone else?* And that can motivate them to work very, very hard because they believe on some unconscious level that if they just earn or achieve great success, their parents, family, friends, or colleagues will finally appreciate them and give them the validation they crave. We all want to feel loved. We all want to be accepted. We all want to feel like we're "good enough." And so I've found that many clients, because of their childhood experiences, have been working day and night to create this image and achieve great success just to show people they deserve attention.

So it becomes a compulsion: "Hey, look at my Ferrari." "Hey, look at my big house." "Hey, look how well I've done." They're looking for a meaningful pat on the head and a "good job" from the proverbial absentee parent. It's a sad way to live. When you remove that desire to prove something to someone, even yourself, it feels easier to make those adjustments, to be okay with spending more time with your kids, on your health, to make time for sleep and exercise, and to take care of your physical and emotional needs.

COMPETING WITH OTHERS

I once had a client who was a very successful attorney—an executive mom rather than an Executive Dad. She had a very similar path in life to many Executive Dads that I've come to know. But her story is remarkable and makes me laugh every time I tell it. She came to me with the classic symptoms of an unbalanced life. She was a high-powered attorney working for a big, "important" company. Her job was essentially to put out fires. They specifically hired her to be on call 24/7—whether she was on vacation or it was three o'clock in the morning. If a client had a problem in New York, China, Europe, or Africa, they'd call her first, and she'd put out that fire.

As a result of her taking on that role, she was paid handsomely. Her job title was one she had dreamed of for years. She was the only woman working with all these other successful men. She wanted to prove she could "hang with the big boys." And yet she was suffering the cost of that role. She had excessive stress, was overweight, didn't have time to exercise, and couldn't relax even on vacation. Even at the beach, she still had to check her phone frequently. She couldn't keep her phone on silent when she went to sleep. So, she never had peace of mind or the ability to fully enjoy the moment. She worked her butt off for over four decades just to get this opportunity.

As the sessions progressed and I got to know her better, I discovered that she didn't really need the money the company was paying her. It paid well, and she was happy with it, but she already had enough saved up to live comfortably for the rest of her life. She was married to an independently wealthy man who told her he'd be comfortable if she quit her job, and they just sailed around the world and had fun. Yet she was hanging on to this job to prove she could "hang with the big boys."

I'm curious when clients tell me things like that, and I wanted to know what made it so important for her to "hang with the big boys." And this part of her story still makes me laugh. She said she had a chip on her shoulder throughout her entire life because she wasn't as bright as her sister. When she was five years old, her parents had her and her sister take an IQ test, and her sister scored five points higher. My client said that throughout her childhood, everything came easier for her sister. Her sister got great grades at school but didn't have to try as hard. My client felt she had to try twice as hard as her sister to keep up and perform as well in school, athletics, or anything else. So, throughout her life, she'd worked harder than everyone else because she felt she had to.

During a subsequent session, it occurred to me to ask her a question about that IQ test. I said, "By the way, when you and your sister took that IQ test, what was your score?" And she said, "Well, my sister scored 159, but I only scored 154."

Pause for laughter.

I quickly googled "IQ by percentile." I was doing my best to stop myself from laughing: This woman had spent half a century thinking she needed to work harder than everyone else because she wasn't smart enough. Yet when I looked up IQ by percentile and saw the results, I said, "So, your sister had an IQ score of 159... Well, this chart says that she's smarter than 99.995% of the population. And with your IQ score of 154, you're 'only' smarter than 99.984% of the population." We both started laughing. Gotta work hard to compensate for that extra 0.011% intelligence gap!

This is a perfect example of an experience we can consciously forget about, but it has profoundly influenced everything we've done for decades. This woman is more intelligent than almost every person on the planet. And not only was she smarter than 99.984% of people,

63

but she also worked harder and put in more hours a week than everyone else throughout her adult life. It's no wonder she was hired by an incredibly valuable company to do an incredibly important job that commanded a huge salary!

During her sessions, we worked through issues related to self-worth. She had been working for this company for about two years. I said, "Well, it seems to me that you've already proven that you can hang with the big boys because you've done it for two years. They haven't fired you. They haven't given you poor reviews. All they've done is compliment you and show you gratitude for the work you've done for them." Yet, in her own mind, she'd been doubting herself. In her own mind, she'd been imagining her peers saying bad things about her behind her back and planning to replace her with someone else, even though her position had been vacant for two years before they found her! She thought quitting her job or scaling back on her hours would be a sign of failure. I helped her understand that, essentially, this was a choice. It wasn't a question of whether or not she was capable of hanging with the big boys. She was clearly more than capable. The real question was, "Is it worth it?"

If you don't have to prove anything to yourself or anybody else, the real question is about whether or not it's worth it to invest so much time and energy, given the tremendous sacrifice and cost. Maybe I'm crazy, but when you already have enough money to retire forever and live a great quality of life, it doesn't make sense to work 60 or 80 hours a week to prove anything to anybody. If you love your work, fantastic! I don't plan to retire 100% as long as I'm alive and kicking. But I won't be working because I'm trying to prove anything. It'll be because I enjoy what I do. I'm proud to report that my client returned within weeks after that session and said she'd already put in her notice. As I write these words, she's traveling around the world with her husband and having a wonderful time in retirement.

BEATING IMPOSTER SYNDROME

Now, there's one more concept I want to talk about that's important for you to consider. I'll put this in context by sharing a story about my wife. When she and I had our daughter Sienna in 2013, my wife decided to take a break from work to devote all her energy and attention to taking care of our newborn baby. She quit her job with Turner Broadcasting System. She was working for Cartoon Network and had a job she loved—designing websites and creating animations. She's incredibly talented. But she gave that up for what she and I believed was the right thing to do when our daughter was born.

She did a wonderful job of that. Then, at one point, we decided it made sense for her to return to work. I agreed to adjust my work schedule so that my daughter would have one of us for all but roughly 20 hours a week. For 20 hours a week, we'd have our daughter with a nanny, and the rest of the time, she would be with us. After being out of the workforce for a while, the landscape of graphic design had changed. My wife was a little worried because the job she had been doing was being replaced by automation. Websites were now being created using templates rather than from scratch by talented people like her. So the old job she was used to wasn't really available anymore.

Shelli applied for nearly 200 positions over the course of a year before she found one she wanted. She wanted a job where she'd be able to work nine to five. The job she accepted was with AT&T. She was working in graphic design, but it was her first time as a project manager. This was a very different corporate environment from any of her previous jobs. One day, she came home from work a bit anxious and upset. She said, "I just don't think I can do this. I'm on these conference calls all day with all these different people, and they're using all these acronyms. I just don't know what they're talking about. I don't know if I can keep up."

With more than a decade of experience as a therapist, I knew a little something about imposter syndrome, and I knew she was experiencing it. Imposter syndrome occurs when someone takes on a job with greater or different responsibilities from what they had previously. Typically, a person in that position has earned it by demonstrating competence or proficiency in their previous position.

The person hiring them gives them an opportunity, expecting they can learn how to do it. Knowing what I did about imposter syndrome and my wife—that she's incredibly hard-working, smart, and very talented as a graphic designer—I told her something I've told clients before. I said, "Honey, I don't think AT&T hired you because you already know the acronyms. I think they hired you because they think you can figure it out." So, my wife went back to her cubicle the next day and began to use sticky notes to decode all the acronyms. She'd write down the acronym and its meaning and plaster these sticky notes around her cubicle. Based on her description, it looked like those serial killer movies where they have yarn between all these different pictures and threads of evidence. But within a few days, she'd decoded all the acronyms so that when she was on conference calls, she could look around and know what they were talking about.

Within a week, she found it easier to keep up. Within a month, she was getting great reviews from her manager. That didn't surprise me because I knew that what my wife brings to the table is why they hired her. She had always been employed, moving from one job to the next, making more money, and taking on increased responsibility. The reason for that is her tremendous work ethic, incredible talent, and creativity. Because of those strengths, she always rises to the top. So I believed in her and knew that. She temporarily forgot that, got a bit nervous, then figured it out, and has been doing well ever since.

The important thing to understand about your own brain is that there are many things you do automatically because of the way your brain is organized, while the survival brain focuses explicitly on problems. Problems require attention because they need to be solved.

Think about when the Wi-Fi goes out at home or work. When the Wi-Fi goes out, everything comes to a halt. Nothing works. Your kids can't access the internet. Nowadays, even your TV doesn't connect anymore. Immediately when the Wi-Fi goes out, it gets 100% of our attention. We have to place all our attention on solving that problem. You either call the company or unplug the modem and plug it back in. You do everything you can to get it working again.

When the Wi-Fi comes back on, how long do you give it attention? How much time do you spend thinking about it when it's working properly? The answer is next to none. Within seconds of it coming back on, you're back to focusing on other things. You're responding to that text message, that email, doing the work, or watching a show. This is a natural byproduct of how the survival brain works. It is constructed not for happiness, gratitude, or peace of mind. It doesn't care about any of those things. Your brain is concerned with avoiding pain and keeping you alive.

No matter how much money you have, you can always think about not having enough. No matter how successful you are, your brain can always imagine, *What if I slide backward? What if someone else passes me up?* No matter how nice your home is, your brain will filter it out so that it's just your home. No matter how talented you are, that level of proficiency will just be normal for you. And where will your attention go? To the areas in which you're struggling. If you're growing and succeeding, running a business or a company, your attention will always focus on the problems that need to be solved, the things you're struggling with, and those things you haven't yet figured out. If you're not aware of the dynamics of imposter syndrome, you could end up thinking less of yourself and feeling anxious. It is essential to counterbalance the survival brain's natural tendencies if you want to elevate from simply surviving to thriving. Thriving is not just about making great money. My definition of thriving is when you and your family are happy and healthy, your bank account is healthy, and when all those things are in good order, then you're really thriving. If any of those things are out of balance, you're really just surviving. So, I want to take you on this journey from surviving to thriving. To do that, we have to teach your survival brain how to think in a different way.

That means instead of focusing so much attention on what's wrong, you have to think about what's right. Instead of being caught up in imagining what could go wrong, you also have to imagine what could go right. Rather than focusing on what you're missing or what your flaws are, you have to become more aware of your strengths and abilities. When you do that, you will increase your sense of self-confidence. That is so important because when you believe in yourself, it's okay to take time off from work. You know that if there's any problem that needs to be solved, you'll be able to handle it. You don't have to be hypervigilant and think about work 24-7. You can pause and give your full attention to your kids, your health, and your spouse, knowing you'll still handle your business responsibilities when the time comes. That comes from having confidence in yourself. It comes from knowing what you have going for you. It comes from knowing you have all the resources, experience, education, wisdom, drive, and work ethic to be successful in your career for the rest of your life.

For the successful executive, the primary difference in whether you give 90% of your attention to work—or 83%, 70%, or even 50% —is the pile of money that accrues in your bank account. But if you've done well in your professional life, it is extremely unlikely that you'll ever be poor. The truth is that you'll never be homeless. If you properly balance your life, you will be safe. You will be secure. In addition to that, you'll likely have happiness, health, a longer life, a greater quality of life, and better relationships and connections with the people you care about the most. To sum it all up, you have to tame your survival brain if you want to do more than survive. You must trust in your ability to use logic and reason to make intelligent decisions rather than emotional decisions. Your logical brain isn't bound by irrational fear and can weigh the potential benefits and consequences in order to make a decision you won't regret.

CHAPTER 6
CONTROL AND CHOICE

irst off, you must accept this one truth: You are in control of your time. From my experience talking to countless clients and Executive Dads, I know the demands on your time can seem never-ending. You might feel like you're not in control, that you have to meet every deadline, attend every meeting, and work long hours to fulfill your responsibilities. However, the truth is that you are in control of every aspect of your life. You're in control of what you do each day, where you go, how you live your life, and how you spend your time. You have the same number of hours and minutes per day as everyone else. Living in a free country means you can decide where you go and what you do. You're not a slave; you can do anything you choose. The truth is that all decisions and choices have benefits and consequences. However, whatever you tell yourself becomes your reality.

When you tell yourself, *I have to do this,* or *I have to do that,* you're creating a reality where you're not in control. You're creating a reality where you're a slave. If you do that often enough, you will feel as though your life is not within your control. However, the reality is that you could choose not to attend that meeting on your calendar. You could flake out, go fishing, play hooky, or stay in bed all day. If you're a successful executive, you don't often make those choices because you know the consequences: losing your status, job, income, and quality of life. So, you make commitments freely and by choice because the benefits of doing them outweigh the benefits of not doing them.

To take control of your life and begin balancing your relationships, health, and career, you have to start making different choices. That comes from first recognizing that these choices exist. Many clients want to lose weight, exercise more, stop drinking, stop smoking, break bad habits, and become healthier. They just struggle to accomplish these things. Remember, you are the CEO of "You, Inc." If you're in charge of running your life like you run a business, then you have to start looking at the big picture. How do you plan your week? How do you plan your month? How do you plan your year or the next ten years to ensure that you achieve the outcomes you define as successful?

If you're running a company, you achieve your goals systematically and intentionally. You create goals, hire a team, plan meetings, and set deadlines. You evaluate your employees. You don't leave it to chance. You're not running a company and just figuring it out on the fly. You don't establish a goal and then go fishing for a few weeks, hoping everything works out. To have success with your company, you have to make plans and be very detailed and specific about how you do things to achieve the desired outcomes. The same goes for your own life. You have to be intentional. If you don't know your ideal outcome, if you don't know what you're striving for, it doesn't give you any clarity on what you need to be doing in the present. Defining success and setting clear goals before taking action is essential. If you have your week planned with meetings, it's with purpose that you perform your executive functions. Of course, you make time in your calendar to wake up, shower, get dressed, have breakfast, and head to the office.

You purposefully plan and set aside time to fulfill responsibilities in your professional life. But what you may not be doing is purposefully planning things like exercise, spending time with your kids, or taking your wife out on a date. If you're not treating your personal life as equally important as your career, it will only get the crumbs that fall off the table. The things we take seriously in life don't get ignored or forgotten. For most executive men thriving in their careers, their personal and family lives get only the leftover scraps of time. That's what you need to correct. I want you to start planning your life in a way that leads to great relationships, great health, and greater success in your professional life. You have to actually *schedule time to work out on your calendar*—right alongside your most important meetings. It means you need to make a priority of *scheduling date nights with your wife* ahead of time. These things go on the calendar because they're important. If they're not on your calendar, it's a sign you don't think of them as being priorities.

Let me give you an example from my personal life. Just before writing this chapter, I had a conversation with a client, and I showed them my calendar. I showed them what my schedule looks like. My client sessions are in blue, my personal tasks are in green, and so on. My workouts and date nights are right there alongside my business appointments. As I sit here on a Friday writing this book, most people are looking forward to their weekends. Most people work long hours Monday through Friday, do some work on the weekends, or spend time with their loved ones. But that's not my schedule. I work long days on Tuesdays and Thursdays. I work a normal day on Friday and a short day on Saturday morning. So I'm only really in the office three and a half days a week, and the other 50% of the week I'm at home. When I'm at home, there is time for some meetings and a bit of work. However, the majority of my time is spent on personal and family duties.

I walk the dogs. I clean the house. I do laundry and dishes because I share a role in maintaining the home, which is equivalent to my wife, who also works full-time. So I'm walking the walk. I'm not some privileged guy sitting in an ivory tower telling you how to live your life. I'm actually living the kind of life that I recommend to others. I live a balanced life in which I create sufficient time for sleep, family, exercise, and all the essential things for long-term success in life. The demand for my services has been so high for roughly 15 years that if I were to work an extra day or two a week, I could increase my bottom line significantly. And frankly, there are some clients I wouldn't lose because they don't want to wait months for a session. But I refuse to sacrifice my personal time. I refuse to sacrifice time with my daughter. I refuse to sacrifice sleep or time going to the gym just to make extra money or finish the book faster.

My personal time is non-negotiable. My time with my daughter is non-negotiable. Getting enough sleep is non-negotiable. These are not things I will sacrifice to fatten my portfolio.

SCHEDULING BALANCE

The first time I had to make this decision was in early 2010. After my appearance on *The Bert Show* (discussed earlier), my phone started ringing off the hook. That first week, the number of phone calls and emails I received from interested potential clients, mostly listeners from the show, was 500% of what I normally received. I went from 10 to 15 calls or emails a week to 75 calls and emails that first week. It wasn't just a temporary bump; that increased demand sustained for many months.

That kind of demand was new to me, so it took a few weeks before I realized I needed to plan some time off for myself—quickly!

I had scheduled myself to work six days a week without two consecutive days off for the next three months. I had painted myself into a corner. So I quickly realized that if I was going to have a week off for vacation or even a few days off to spend with friends or do things for myself, I had to plan it far in advance. By the end of that year, I had planned and taken several vacations and organized my schedule in a way that ensured I had time for my voice to recover, time to rest, time to go to the gym, and time to balance my life so that when I was working with my clients, I was at my very best. This is something many executive men fail to do. They jump into the situation, accept the job, move up the ladder, and are on the path to success, but they don't stop to plan or think, *How will this affect me in the long term? What will this do to me if I keep working these many hours?*

Your business or the company that pays you—whether your own or a big corporation—will not tell you to back off. If you're waiting for someone to step in and prioritize your needs, don't hold your breath. No one will come along and tell you to take time off to spend with your family or take care of your health (unless your performance is slipping or you've become an annoyance). The level of commitment you have to that job and the productivity you create within your job is something that stockholders, the board, or your superior will be very happy with. It's in their interest that you work as much as humanly possible. They'll keep giving you more work as long as you're getting things done. It's up to you to decide how much is enough. It's up to you to set boundaries.

If you are going to balance your life, it's a decision that you alone make. You will have to take the initiative to create balance in your life. There will always be more work for the executive, but your kids won't be kids forever. Each and every day, if you're the leader of a company, there will always be undone items on your to-do list. A job never ends for an executive. I joke that my to-do list has to-do lists from different coaches I work with or people who work for me, things I need to do or create or give to others for things to move forward in the business. Yet every day, at a certain point in time, I turn that part of my brain off and spend time with my daughter or sit in bed and read a book to wind down. No matter how much you do, your work will never be "done."

This is something you have to accept. And what will be the potential consequence of this strategy? Well, it could be the loss of a client, a financial loss, upsetting someone or letting others down... or all of the above. To deny this would be dishonest. But that potential consequence has to be balanced by what is gained. And what you gain is your sanity, better physical and mental health, and being more present with yourself and your loved ones. All choices have benefits and consequences. You have to zoom out and look at the whole picture instead of looking at the potential negative consequences in a vacuum.

MANAGING YOUR TOOLS

Another factor in creating balance in your life is controlling your technology. The phone in your hand or beside you right now, buzzing or beeping with reminders, can be a helpful tool but also an annoyance that prevents you from properly focusing your time and energy. It's very important to do simple things like putting your phone in "do not disturb" mode, placing it face down, or turning it off for specific periods so you can be fully present and focus on what's happening at the moment. Otherwise, while you're hanging out with your kids, they'll see a guy who's present in the room but completely ignoring them while staring at a screen. Your wife and kids will get the message that you have more important things to do than give them your attention. You have to imagine things from their perspective.

If you don't control your device, it will control you. If you allow the reminders to keep buzzing and beeping, you will be a slave to that device. You'll have to look at it and respond to messages, not when it's convenient for you, but when it's convenient for the other person reaching out to you. Because you are in control of yourself and your time, you must control your technology with purpose and intelligence. Set aside time to respond to messages when it's convenient for you so you are not constantly distracted and shifting your attention from one thing to another, resulting in subpar performance. This isn't just about being a great father, a great husband, and staying in shape. This is about you being at your peak at all times so that whatever you do, whether personal, family, or work-related, you do it to the best of your ability. You're rested, energized, clear-headed, focused, and on point. If that sounds impossible, you need to look in the mirror. You decide who you are and what you do. No one else decides that for you.

Your actions flow from your priorities and values. If you have a voice in your mind that says, *My job, career, and income define me,* your career will supersede anything related to your health, marriage, or children. Therefore, it's important to examine yourself and your priorities and values. It's a helpful exercise to write down your priorities. Think about it. What would be at the top of your list? Is it financial security? Your health? Your family? What do you consider your top priorities in life? If you've never written them down or thought about it in great detail, your actions may be flowing from a place that's completely illogical or irrational. Self-examination requires time free from distraction. It's crucial to sit down, think clearly, and decide how to best use your time to fulfill your responsibilities based on your priorities and values.

The story you create, the story you tell yourself, is your reality. If you tell yourself, *I have to respond to this text,* or *My business will collapse if I take a break,* that will feel real for you. Conversely, if you tell yourself, *My time with my kids is non-negotiable,* or *I can do*

77

anything I want, or *I will always be secure financially,* that will feel real for you as well. The story you tell yourself will become your reality. So it's important to decide what reality you want to experience. What do you want your life to be like? If you want to be free and secure, you have to tell yourself, *I am free,* and *I am secure.* It may take some repetition before it really sinks in, but that is the reality you will create and the reality where you will live.

CONTROLLING EMOTIONS

I often talk about emotional independence, a concept that became apparent after years of therapy. I realized that all the issues my clients sought help for were related to emotional control in one way or another. Whether they were overeating, smoking, or having extramarital affairs, all these negative behaviors sprang from an undesirable emotional state. I want to talk about how hypnosis, when used properly, can give you the control of your emotions necessary to free yourself from dependence on things like alcohol, drugs, food, cigarettes, or other destructive behaviors. I want you to achieve *in*dependence rather than dependence. Dependence is when you need something outside of yourself. Independence is when you're in charge.

There was a time when I used alcohol to numb my feelings of anxiety or nervousness. I used things like movies or sporting events to make myself temporarily feel happier, to forget about my problems or worries. Yet, after my first experience with hypnosis, I developed an increased ability to make myself feel good through shifts in my thinking and consciousness. I realized it was crazy that people rarely think with intent. We hear a song on the radio, and it reminds us of a memory from 20 years ago. Then, 10 seconds later, we forget about that as we see a billboard while driving that reminds us of a meeting later that day. The realization that our thought patterns are so random, combined with the connection between our thoughts and emotional state, struck me as absolutely crazy!

It was crazy that you'd have a good day if good things happened to you and a bad day if bad stuff happened to you. Your emotional state would be entirely dependent on factors outside of your control. If you don't think with intent, you're a slave to your past programming and triggers in your present environment. You could hear a random song, be reminded of a breakup, then spend hours thinking about the worst moments and feeling depressed. If you haven't become aware of this, whether it's the thoughts you think about yourself or the thoughts you think about the world, the vast majority of them are programmed. What I mean by "programmed" is that they were programmed into your mind through your experiences in life. The things you experienced when you were young (formed beliefs), those beliefs become thought patterns that remain in your mind each day. Thoughts like, *I don't have willpower,* or *I'm an all-or-nothing person* are not logically true, but they feel true because they've been there for a long time, are familiar, and you've heard them a thousand times. The problem with letting your programmed thoughts run on autopilot is that you'll just feel however your programmed thoughts make you feel and respond to triggers in your environment like a trained seal rather than responding with intelligence, purpose, and intent.

You achieve emotional independence when you can control your emotional state through the purposeful management of your thoughts. Yes, it takes practice. Some people accomplish this by journaling. Some people write gratitude journals every single day. However, creating lasting changes in your thoughts can be very difficult and take a long time unless you're using hypnosis as a tool. That's why I recommend using hypnosis to change your thought patterns. It's the fastest and most efficient way to create changes in your thoughts and emotions that create changes in your actions and behaviors and, thus, truly lasting changes in your life.

KNOWING YOURSELF

I want to talk about self-confidence. Many executive men I've spoken to are initially very hesitant to make these changes. They become aware during our sessions that their life is out of balance. They realize they could be better fathers, spend more time with their families, and take better care of their health. But the hesitancy comes from uncertainty about their ability to maintain their career success if they begin to make these changes. Establishing rock-solid self-confidence is crucial if you're going to be an elite Executive Dad. Confidence comes from memories of competence. To be confident about something, it's important to remember that you've done it before. If I ask you, "Are you confident you can drive your car from one place to another?" your answer would probably be "Yes." The reason is that you have memories of driving your car successfully from one place to another. However, if I were to ask, "Are you confident you can spend more time with your kids, create a better relationship with your wife, exercise regularly, and still perform at a high level in your career?" you might not feel so confident because you don't have memories of doing those things consistently.

There's a big difference between knowledge and awareness. Knowledge represents all the information that exists within your brain. Your brain has information you've taken in through your senses throughout your entire life, including things you learned in school about history and mathematics. The popular game show *Are You Smarter Than a Fifth Grader?* demonstrates this phenomenon clearly. The show pits fifth graders against adults, using questions about things the fifth graders have learned very recently and that the adults may have learned 20 or 30 years ago. It's funny, but it makes sense that the fifth graders have an easier time answering some of these questions because they're more recent. The problem is that there are many things you know that you haven't recalled in years. When you forget important things you know, you can feel lost. What's important about hypnosis is that you can program your mind purposefully and create changes in your consciousness to ensure you not only know but also remember the important information at the appropriate time. As I like to say, "It's not what you know; it's when you know it." If you want to remember the right information at the right time, it's helpful to use hypnosis to train your brain. The goal is to have greater emotional control through self-hypnosis training.

When I refer to "self-hypnosis," I'm talking about learning to enter that optimal state of relaxation independently. In the field of hypnotherapy, we say, "All hypnosis is self-hypnosis." Whether you're sitting in a hypnotherapist's office, listening to a recording of a hypnosis session, or just sitting comfortably in your favorite chair and closing your eyes, you're always in control. You can either listen and relax or stay in a consciously aware state. When you're practicing self-hypnosis, you are either listening to an audio recording of a hypnotist like myself, or you are remembering a time in which you were hypnotized and allowing your body to respond with muscle memory to create the same response of mental and physical relaxation you experienced. Practicing self-hypnosis consistently will train your mind and body to be relaxed instead of anxious or stressed. Deep relaxation is the opposite of tension. The more deeply relaxed you are, the less anxious or stressed you are. Practicing self-hypnosis consistently will establish a new norm. Your baseline emotional state will be calmer, more relaxed, and more peaceful.

Achieving that state ultimately leads to more than simple relaxation. It puts you in a state where you become a better listener, so when you receive suggestions, they stick. You begin to notice differences in your consciousness throughout the day. That's something

I'm going to explain in more detail in the next chapter. Remember that it's very important that you know yourself. You have to know your strengths, resources, and accomplishments. If you're an Executive Dad, you probably take for granted that you've already accomplished more than most people ever will. Most people never become executives or CEOs. Most people never start their own businesses. Many people, frankly, don't have families. Many people don't get married. Many people don't have kids. So the truth is, if you're reading this book, you've accomplished quite a lot already. If you're not feeling very confident about your ability to do what I'm suggesting, it probably means you're not giving yourself enough credit.

We all have memories of success. One story that I want to share with you puts this in context. I told you about my experience with improvisational comedy. I spent six years doing improv at Whole World Theatre in Atlanta, Georgia, between 1999 and 2005. In 2005, I decided to retire from that theater because I knew my business needed my full attention, and I couldn't devote five nights a week to something that wasn't going to be my career. So, I left improv comedy and worked full-time at Turner Broadcasting System while trying to grow my practice in the evenings and on weekends.

Somehow, word got around at Turner that I had experience as a performer, and in 2006, I was asked to host an event at the Fox Theatre in Atlanta. It was a family event for The Cartoon Network, which was launching a new cartoon starring Andre 3000 from OutKast. There would be between 2,000 and 3,000 people in attendance. I'd never hosted or been on stage in front of that many people before. The biggest crowd I'd ever performed for was a couple hundred people. Yet when they approached me about this opportunity, I immediately said yes. (I have a habit of doing that.) I said yes because I knew something at that point in time. I had a lot of confidence in myself from performing improv all those years. I thought, *It's the same thing. There are more people, but I'm on a stage, and I will be asked to entertain them and make them laugh.* I'd done that many times before, so I took the job. I remember showing up at the Fox Theatre that night and being very excited. I had my own dressing room. I prepared, got dressed, and put on my microphone.

I went out in front of this audience of thousands. Atlanta's Fox Theatre is immense and beautiful. I'd been there many times before as an audience member, so it was surreal to be on the stage looking out. During the course of an hour or two, I was in charge of keeping everyone engaged and entertained. I asked them questions, told jokes, did funny voices, and gave away prizes. Everything was going perfectly. At a certain point, when my time was up, I thanked the audience, went backstage, and handed my microphone to the stage manager.

As I headed toward the dressing room, the stage manager tapped me on the shoulder. He said, "Hey, I've got the director telling me we need you to go back out there and do five more minutes." I said, "Sure, no problem. I'll go back out there and do a little more of what I was doing..." and he quickly replied, "No, the director said the marching band from the local high school is about to come down the aisle, and we need everyone to stay in their seats. You can't go out there with the audience and do the stuff you were doing before. And we need you to go out there right now." It was almost like in the movies where you see a character being shoved out through the curtain onto a stage. He gave me a hand mic, and I quickly walked back toward the audience. Just imagine walking out onto the stage at the Fox Theatre in front of thousands of people, and the first thought that goes through your head is, *What the hell am I gonna do?*

I recall that moment so vividly. I never panicked, but I did have that thought. But within less than a second, two different thoughts entered my mind. One was a picture, and one was a voice. The picture that flashed in my mind was of my improv theater as it looked from the stage, where I'd performed in hundreds of shows. The voice in my mind said *You can do this.* So I took a breath and continued walking on stage. Over the next several minutes, I figured it out. To be honest, I don't remember exactly what I said. I know that pop star Chris Brown was performing that night, and whenever I said his name, the audience screamed like he was Michael Jackson. It really startled me at first because I had no idea who Chris Brown was before that night! So, I might have said his name a couple more times to get some cheers. All I remember is that at a certain point, I told the audience, "Thanks again! Good night for real this time!" Then, I headed backstage. As I handed the microphone to the stage manager, his jaw dropped, and he gave me a puzzled look. I said, "What?" And he looked at me and said, "That was exactly five minutes." I hadn't been counting.

I learned something very powerful that night. Number one, in that moment of uncertainty, my brain had been programmed to remind me of something incredibly important. Although I was in a new location, doing something I hadn't done before in that way, I had literally hundreds of hours of improvisational experience, and I was being asked to improvise! I had a voice in my mind that reminded me of that by saying, *You can do this.* So, at that point in time, I'd been involved in hypnosis for half a decade, and I'd done so much self-hypnosis that I had programmed my brain to remind me of what I needed to know when I needed to know it. The other thing I learned from that night was that I have a pretty good internal clock that told me when five minutes was up. The fact that it was exactly five minutes was perhaps a bit lucky.

Another relevant story is from early January 2011, when I appeared on *Swift Justice with Nancy Grace.* It was a courtroom show similar to *Judge Judy* that Nancy Grace, the longtime CNN Headline News anchor, was hosting. Nancy was the judge. I was asked to participate as an expert forensic hypnotist. The case involved a woman accused of damaging $2,000 worth of computer equipment belonging to her boyfriend. The accusation was that she destroyed the computer equipment in a drunken rage, but she had no memory of doing it. The producer who contacted me asked if I could hypnotize her to recall what happened. I remember replying, "So you're asking me if I can hypnotize a woman accused of a civil offense to confess on camera in front of an audience of millions and everyone she knows on television?"

He replied, "Well, when you say it that way, it sounds really hard!"

I laughed and said it wouldn't be the easiest thing I'd ever done. But at the time of that phone call, two things came to mind. First, I wanted to be on television. After abandoning my previous career in broadcasting, I dreamed of being on television as a hypnotherapist. I thought it would be poetic justice. I could spread the word about hypnosis, get some national exposure, and grow my practice. The other thing I recalled was that I'd had one client previously who'd asked me to do something similar. My client was a 16-year-old girl whose parents allowed her to drink alcohol with her friends on her 16th birthday. Not a great idea in my book, but it's what her parents decided to do.

Predictably, something really bad happened that night. The next day, her friends all accused her of taking a friend's car for a drunken joy ride down the street and crashing into another parked car. My client blacked out and had no memory of doing it. She wondered if one of her friends was responsible and the others were covering for her and blaming my client. Sadly, as a result of that incident, she lost all her friends and transferred to another school across town to live with her grandmother. On the date of her session, she came in with her grandmother and told me she genuinely wanted to know what happened that night so she could have closure and move on.

So I hypnotized her, and she clearly recalled driving down the street and crashing into a parked car. After the session, she realized she was responsible for what had happened. That gave her some closure and peace of mind and allowed her to move on with her life, perhaps a bit wiser. I'd only done this type of memory recovery on that one occasion, but the awareness of having done it even once successfully, along with my desire to spread the word about hypnosis, inspired me to take a calculated risk. I decided to roll the dice, put myself out there, and appear on national television. So, I appeared on the Nancy Grace show. I hypnotized the woman to recall what happened. She confessed on camera, and everything worked exquisitely well. As a side note, I helped her with her alcohol problem, which never appeared in the episode. She expressed a willingness to cooperate with the hypnosis and a desire to know the truth about what happened, so I gave her some words of inspiration to make better decisions moving forward.

The key takeaway here is that we don't take advantage of opportunities like that unless we remember how capable we are and that we've had success in the past. It's not what you know; it's when you know it. Hypnosis can help you program yourself to remember what you need to know when it truly matters so you can be in an optimal state to take advantage of life's opportunities.

When you remember what you've accomplished, you have the courage to take on something new that may be challenging and involve some risk. When you remember how capable you are, how successful you've been, how intelligent you are, and what resources you have at your disposal, you can take the courageous next step in your journey toward being an amazing, elite Executive Dad.

One thing to keep on your radar when it comes to knowing yourself is a certain flaw in human perception. I've spoken earlier in this book about the negativity bias, our tendency to focus on negative stimuli more than positive stimuli, which has been well-documented in many studies. When it comes to your self-perception, the problem could be that because of the negativity bias, you're more aware of what you perceive to be your flaws and shortcomings or mistakes that you've made and not as aware of your strengths, positive qualities, or accomplishments. Problems require attention, whereas strengths and accomplishments don't. So, it's very important to recognize that if you want to feel confident and strong, you have to change your internal focus to become more aware of your strengths and less focused on your nitpicks.

To move forward, transform your life, and create that kind of balance, it's crucial to have a clear vision of your goals and what your ideal life looks like. Just as when running a company, you have to have a vision of what success will look like. One of the great things about hypnosis is that when you're in the hypnotic state, your ability to visualize and imagine is enhanced. With clients, I often put them in a trance and tap into their creativity and imagination. The emotion that comes from those pictures and movies that you imagine begins to create the roadmap where you see yourself as the husband and father you want to be, playing with your kids, having more intimacy in your relationship, being in better shape, and having a better quality of life. They create the incentive and energy required to do what's necessary to achieve those goals.

Changing your self-perception creates an increased awareness of your strengths, abilities, and positive qualities. You're reminding yourself that your value is not attached to your accomplishments. I fully believe that your value as a human being is intrinsic. It is not associated with how much money you have, what your job status is, how big your home is, or anything else. Your value as a human being is intrinsic. Your career accomplishments, your bank account, your possessions, your quality of life—these things are important, but they are not related to your value as a human being. It is important to treat yourself as you would treat someone you love. Whether it's your best friend, your spouse, your kids, or a close family member, the rule is if you wouldn't treat them that way, then you don't treat yourself that way. If you wouldn't ask or demand someone you love to work 80 hours a week and sacrifice their health and relationships for the betterment of a company, then you don't ask that of yourself. If you wouldn't tell someone else, "You're an idiot. You're stupid. You're no good," then don't say those things to yourself. You create a greater and healthier perception of yourself by treating yourself the same way you would treat someone you love. This may sound a little woo-woo or touchy-feely, but after 20 years as a therapist, I assure you it's perfectly healthy and reasonable to love and respect yourself. When you do so, you can achieve more than you ever dreamed you could in the past.

CHAPTER 7
A POWERFUL TOOL

Now, you don't have to take my word for it that hypnosis is a powerful tool. A little research will reveal that there are thousands of university and clinical studies on its effectiveness. Hypnotherapy has been part of our society for decades, dating back to at least the 1940s and 1950s, and probably much further in reality. In the United States, since the 1950s, doctors, dentists, and medical professionals have used hypnosis for various purposes, from helping cancer patients heal from their therapies to aiding post-surgery recovery and even as a substitute for anesthesia in patients allergic to anesthetics. Yes, it is possible to undergo a root canal or surgery without anesthetic and feel no pain simply by being put under hypnosis by a trained professional.

I know hypnosis is not the main reason you're reading this book. You're interested in learning how to better run your life for the reasons I've discussed. However, hypnosis is an important tool for implementing and creating that kind of life. You can understand something logically, but that doesn't mean it will change your life. Many books provide great insights that readers think, *Wow, this makes sense,* but nothing changes because our consciousness quickly forgets. I don't want that to be your experience with this book. I want you to retain and act upon this knowledge. I want you to change your life.

Think of hypnosis as the tool and delivery system we use to implement changes in your thinking that result in changes in your emotions, fueling important changes in your behaviors. I'll start by telling a little story about when I was first hypnotized. Like most people, being a hypnotherapist wasn't on my radar. I didn't even know it was a profession when I went to college. I attended the University of Miami in 1993, aiming for a career in sports journalism. Four years later, I graduated and moved to Atlanta to work for CNN Sports Illustrated. My career was off to a great start. However, as you may recall from my story earlier in this book, it didn't go exactly as planned.

On a cold January day in Atlanta, Georgia, in 2001, I stumbled into a hypnotherapist's office, ostensibly for help with performance anxiety. During that session, something magical happened. I experienced a profound relaxation that I'd never felt before. I want you to understand what hypnosis actually is and how you know when you're experiencing it. Hypnosis can produce the deepest feelings of relaxation known to man. I felt my toes and fingers tingling and becoming numb. At times, it felt as though I was completely detached from my body. My heart rate slowed, my breathing deepened, and I felt completely peaceful. I had moments of awareness of being on a beach and enjoying some pretty imagery. I had wonderful moments of just existing, with no past or future, just a profound feeling of contentment.

What resulted from that experience was a powerful shift in my consciousness. I felt as though I had been unplugged from *The Matrix*. I felt like I'd awakened from a dream where all my thoughts had been random. I realized that throughout my life, I'd never really been thinking on purpose. There were times when I'd been introspective and focused my attention purposefully to study for a test or prepare for a meeting, but I never really recognized the connection between my thoughts and my emotional state before that crucial awakening. If you're not thinking purposefully or with intent, you will not be truly independent. That means you're dependent, like I was at the time, on things outside of yourself to change your emotional state.

Hypnotherapy has been practiced for thousands of years, and modern research on hypnosis is well-documented. Yet, in today's culture, it still feels like something outside the mainstream. One reason for that is the existence of stage hypnosis. For most people, their first exposure to hypnosis is via stage shows. That's true for me; I saw two such shows while in college, which piqued my curiosity. A decade later, when I studied hypnotherapy, my improv comedy experience fueled a renewed interest in stage hypnosis. I thought it was a perfect combination of my comedic background and my newfound hypnosis skills. By the summer of 2003, only a few months after I completed my hypnotherapy certification training, I was already performing my first comedy stage hypnosis shows for live audiences.

The first thing to understand about stage hypnosis is that it's a real phenomenon. The people hypnotized in these shows are not "faking it." They fully participate in an experience that leads to a tremendously good time for both participants and the audience. Hypnosis is a cooperative endeavor. It's not about control. People are hypnotized because they've willingly volunteered to participate and followed the hypnotist's instructions. This is true whether it's in my office during a therapy session or in a comedy club during a stage performance. The individual has to follow the hypnotist's instructions to relax and get into the state. Speaking as a former participant and the hypnotist, I can tell you that once you're in that state of deep relaxation, you feel wonderful. It's the opposite of feeling anxious or stressed.

For most people, it's quite strange to be totally relaxed and in a deep state of comfort while in front of an audience of strangers. Usually, people are very self-conscious in that setting. So when the hypnotist suggests predictably silly things to his hypnotized subjects, they're responding to his suggestions not because they're puppets he controls but because it's part of an unspoken agreement: Follow the hypnotist's suggestions, and you'll feel incredibly relaxed and have a wonderful time. The suggestions given are in accordance with their expectations for that experience. Remember that when people participate in a stage or comedy hypnosis show, they're not doing so because they've been tricked. They weren't expecting a group therapy session where they suddenly found themselves dancing with a broom. They volunteer knowing they'll be asked to do silly things and are ready to have some fun. So when those types of suggestions are given, it's not a surprise and is fully congruent with their expectations. People cannot be forced to do things that are against their morals and values in that context.

Although stage hypnosis can create misconceptions, it also introduces many people to hypnosis for the first time. It was how I first encountered hypnosis as a college student. It was also how my lovely wife first experienced hypnosis on a cruise ship. When you understand the dynamics of how hypnosis works, stage hypnosis makes sense, as does hypnotherapy. The context determines how people respond. When you're in my office for a hypnotherapy session, you won't quack like a duck or bark like a dog because that's not why you're here. But as long as the suggestions you receive are congruent with your desires, you will accept and respond to those suggestions. As a result, changes will take place, and you'll experience benefits.

The state of hypnosis makes you a better listener and puts you in a state where you can program your thoughts in a better, more purposeful way. We are creatures of habit in word and action. Hypnosis allows us to create new thought patterns that benefit us—patterns that create emotions, enabling us to be in the best state to fulfill our potential.

TAMING YOUR BRAIN

I often describe hypnosis as a tool to help people "tame their survival brain." Your brain is programmed first and foremost for survival, and everything it does automatically is geared toward keeping you alive. Whether it's worries about money compelling you to save or concerns about your children's well-being compelling you to keep tabs on them and ensure their safety, all these automated thoughts help ensure survival. However, none of them create happiness or peace of mind.

To achieve a balanced life, to not only survive but thrive, you have to tame your survival brain. What I do with hypnosis on a personal level, and what I do with this knowledge, is to create thought patterns within my mind that help me remain in a good state. It's funny because, as I've discussed, no matter how much money you make, you can always worry about losing it. No matter how great your quality of life is, you can always take it for granted. I have implemented some strategies personally so that when my survival brain begins to worry me, it doesn't disrupt my state or create stress. For example, if my business is having a slower week or revenue is down from the previous month, my survival brain will kick in and say, *Hey, what's going on? Why are you having a down month? What if this trend continues?* But I've become mindful of my internal dialogue. I've become aware of my survival brain and what it's trying to do for me. I've programmed another voice to respond. That voice says something to the effect of, *Relax, you're safe.*

I remind myself that I'm not under threat, my life is not in danger, and my survival is not in danger. I remind myself that no matter what happens in my business today, this week, this month, or even this year, I will not only survive but thrive in the future because of the skills, talents, resources, and work ethic I possess. I remember what I've already accomplished and that I can overcome adversity and obstacles. I remind myself of how much better I'm doing now than I was in the past and give myself a healthy perspective.

Perspective is one of the most important things we can change because of the brain's tendency to acclimate to new and greater levels of success. You can do a perspective shift. One of my perspective shifts is basic but incredibly powerful. If you're a dad, here's something I know you can relate to powerfully. As you know, I have an 11-year-old daughter named Sienna. I've talked about her at great length. I know from experiences with clients, family, and friends that if your child had a terminal illness, you would sacrifice everything you had—every possession, every penny, even your last breath—just to make that child healthy and well again. You'd give up your house, millions of dollars, and everything you owned just so your child could be healthy. Sometimes, I remember this and think about how I would give away everything without hesitation. It makes my present problems seem small. That's a very powerful perspective shift.

This is very important because if you're going to make changes in your life and have new experiences that present new challenges, it's crucial to remember that the problems you're focusing on are very small compared to those you could be experiencing or that others are dealing with in this world right now.

Another perspective shift has to do with your financial or career position. Who are you comparing yourself to? Are you comparing yourself to those in the top 1% of income earners above you, or neck-and-neck with you in your industry? Or are you comparing yourself to the average Joe? Competitiveness can be a powerful motivator, but one of its byproducts is stress, which must be properly harnessed. If you're an Executive Dad, you're doing better than 99% or more of the people on this planet, including 99% of those other dads out there. If you're worried about falling behind others in the executive world, you're losing valuable perspective. You have to remind yourself that you're killing it at work and in your career. With the knowledge, tools, and resources you possess, you will always be able to survive, and without all the excessive stress, you'll always be able to thrive.

BECOMING MINDFUL

One of the things we need to do to tame the survival brain is to create a different type of trigger that helps you become aware that your brain is worrying about things that aren't useful. I call this "disciplined worry." As a responsible man, I know that, at times, I actually have a responsibility to worry. At times, I have to think about my family, our health, and my business, plan for things, and address problems. But what's important is that I only think about these things when it's useful. I first have to ask myself when my brain begins to worry: *Is this something that I can control?* Next, I have to ask myself, *Is now the right time to address this?* Many of the things we worry about, we can't control at all. You might worry about what some other company or fellow employee will do, the state of the economy, who will be elected president, or what new policies will be implemented. Depending on your line of work, some of those worrying thoughts can only have a limited impact on your actual behaviors. So it's important to distinguish between thoughts worthy of your time and when it's useful to think about them.

Remember that the purpose of worrying thoughts is to inspire action to prevent bad outcomes. It's only useful to think about problems in a way that leads to action or solution. If you think about things you can't control, you need to shift your attention and tell yourself *That's not my problem* or *Now's not the time.*

When you decide that thought isn't useful or productive, the next question is, "What should I think of next?" Here's what I suggest: There are times when it's important to give your attention to the present moment. Whether you're focusing on a problem at work, in a meeting, or having dinner with your family, there are times when it's important to be fully present. Give your child your full attention, give your wife your full attention, or focus on the task at hand. If you're out fishing, give that your full attention! There are other times when you could be driving in your car and free to drift in your thoughts. You don't have to focus on pushing the gas pedal at the appropriate time or turning the steering wheel to move onto one street or another because those things happen automatically. When you do something automatically, your thoughts can go in various directions. You can remember the past, think about the future, or do an inventory of your present life and be grateful for the things going well. For simplicity, I put these thoughts into three categories—past, present, and future. When you find yourself worrying about something not within your control, or it's not the right time to address it, you can shift your focus to a memory that creates a good feeling, a future event you're looking forward to, or something right here in the present. Maybe it's nice that you're driving a car you picked out. You chose the color, you enjoy how it responds, and you appreciate the experience of driving that car.

There are many things you can give your attention to that will calm your mind, relax your body, and keep you in a resourceful state so you're not endlessly problem-solving and worrying in a way that creates a need for alcohol, food, drugs, or other destructive behaviors to change your emotional state. Taming your survival brain means thinking more and more with purpose and intent and taking responsibility for the content of your thoughts to exercise greater control over how you feel.

When used properly, hypnosis can create powerful shifts in consciousness. If I'm working with a client who wants to eat healthier, one simple suggestion I give them is to think about how they're going to feel after eating a certain type of food before deciding what to eat. Most people don't think about it until it's too late, when they wish they'd eaten something healthier. If you think about the consequences before you make the choice, it makes it easier to make a good choice that you won't regret. I use hypnosis to remind people of the right information at the right time. There are unlimited suggestions that will create a shift in your consciousness and inspire a different emotional response, leading to better behavior.

Hypnosis can also be used to realign your values and priorities. When you and I talk during a session about your values and priorities, you may discover that you're out of alignment—that you've been prioritizing work above health, family, and children. With your cooperation and willingness, I can help you change how those priorities are aligned so that you begin to feel better about redirecting your energy, time, and resources in a way that respects your true values and priorities.

Hypnosis can also eliminate negative or limiting beliefs. You may have beliefs related to your work, family, or career that cause you to act in ways that lead to adverse outcomes. You might believe that if you don't work 80 hours a week, you won't be able to hang with the big boys. You may think your needs aren't as important as others. If you have a belief like that, it will massively interfere with your ability to balance your life and become the kind of dad your kids need, or the husband your wife deserves.

Hypnosis can also eliminate fear. Typically, fear comes from mental pictures of negative events or outcomes or your internal dialogue. We all talk to ourselves. As long as you're not doing so out loud on a crowded city street, you're like most people. It's an internal conversation where you can really freak yourself out. *What if I fail? What if my wife leaves me? I'm going to lose everything.* And we all visualize, whether consciously or unconsciously. You may have pictures or movies in your mind of catastrophes unfolding. It's natural. Hypnosis can eliminate those pictures and change your internal dialogue to eliminate fearful feelings. If you look at my reviews on Google, you'll see that many of my clients report their fear of flying, driving, heights, or other things disappeared quickly as a result of our sessions.

Hypnosis can also instill mindfulness via suggestions that help you become more present. I frequently do this with my Executive Dads, who report difficulty giving their full attention to their wives and kids due to persistent intrusive thoughts about work. They drift into "responsibility" thoughts or keep checking their phone. They start thinking about what's on their to-do list for tomorrow or what's going to happen next week. They're usually living in the future instead of the present. It's not voluntary; these thoughts have been programmed to keep coming into their mind. I use hypnosis to help them become more mindful and focused on the information coming in through their senses. The point is to be aware of the person talking to you across the dinner table and actually listen to what your child is saying so you can respond in a helpful, appropriate, or useful way. It's about programming yourself to be mindful. This also has the added benefit of you feeling better and being happier! The ultimate goal isn't to be perfect. (My wife and friends will assure you I'm quite imperfect!) The goal is to experience the greatest amount of happiness while living a life in accordance with your values.

If I simply told you to be mindful, be present, don't be afraid, and assess your values and priorities, you might understand the logic, but it'd be very difficult to do all that on your own through conscious willpower. Your programmed thoughts would dominate, making it an uphill battle. So, I can't emphasize enough that hypnosis is an essential tool to implement necessary changes. Remember, you can change your priorities. You are in control of your phone and technology. You can redefine your identity and how you think of yourself. And you can use hypnosis to ensure that you remain aware of the truth—that you will always be able to provide for yourself and your family. You will always be able to thrive in this world and your life.

CHAPTER 8
REDEFINING LEGACY

've shared some core problems inherent in being an Executive Dad and some tools to implement important changes in your life that are practical, proven, and effective. Now, I want to talk about legacy. When I speak with Executive Dads, legacy is frequently a topic that is quick to come up. A recent client spoke about leaving enough wealth so his children, grandchildren, and great-grandchildren never have to worry about money. I understand that desire completely. Who wouldn't want unlimited wealth to take care of their family, ensuring their needs are met, and they never have to worry about money, bills, or access to health care? However, this desire has inherent flaws. I want to start by sharing my experiences with my parents.

As I mentioned, my parents prioritized spending time with their kids, making us the focal point of their lives. As a result, my brother, sister, and I are all happily married, love our kids, are mentally balanced, and live happy and productive lives. We all have careers that make us happy. We're not going to inherit from our parents, and we're fine with that. They empowered us to make our own way in the world. They made great sacrifices to put us through the best schools they could afford. All three of us went to private Catholic schools before heading off to the college of our choice. Our parents co-financed our college tuition while we earned scholarships and took out student loans.

Our parents sacrificed heavily in their personal lives to give us the best possible education. They invested in us rather than the stock market, a bigger home, material possessions, or fancy vacations. As a result, they have three kids who are happy, educated, and thriving as adults. That's their legacy. I know other parents didn't make the same choices and didn't invest as much time or money in their children's education, and their kids aren't thriving as we are. As I've grown older and become a parent, I appreciate the wisdom in my parents' choices. For them, it wasn't about leaving behind a huge pile of money. It was about the importance of family connection and making sure their kids knew they were loved.

This has influenced my definition of "legacy" deeply. I've met countless clients who inherited tremendous wealth yet came to me for help with depression, addiction to alcohol and drugs, or both. These people have all the money in the world but lacked the happiness and joy that my siblings and I have. Initially, I found this perplexing and then fascinating. Now, after two decades as a therapist, it makes perfect sense. Our feelings have little to do with logic and reason and are instead a result of our programmed thoughts.

We develop a certain way of thinking based on our childhood experiences. No matter how much money our parents give us, if they don't give us their time, we tend to feel unimportant. The resulting anxiety, sadness, and emotional damage from not feeling "good enough" can last a lifetime. Unlimited financial resources can lead people to make costly mistakes and become involved with drugs, alcohol, and unhealthy relationships.

Regarding legacy, the two most valuable things you possess are time and money. We all know the expression "time is money." So which will you give more of to your children? If you have great wealth, it's easy to throw money at your kids, buy them things, take them on fancy vacations, and get them the nicest clothes. In the short term, these things can make your children happy. But ask yourself, *Are these things as valuable as my time?* You may have unlimited wealth, but no one has unlimited time. Your time is more valuable than your money. As I mentioned earlier, I've sacrificed roughly half a million dollars in the first ten years of my daughter's life just to spend one extra day per week with her. How much will you sacrifice to spend more time with your kids?

Another question is, *How will my children remember me when I'm gone?* Will they remember the stuff you gave them, the vacations, or their experiences with you? Many clients have described their fathers as "great" but also "not around much." I find that incredibly sad. But I'm biased—I take things to the extreme in the other direction. I turned my former career into a hobby. Back in college, I fell in love with making videos. While studying broadcast journalism, I learned how to shoot and edit videos. This was long before smartphones and iMacs. I enjoyed capturing moments and putting them together in a way that would last. After Sienna was born, I took pictures and videos of everything she did, then edited all those moments into watchable movies. Every year on her birthday, our family watches a film of her previous year that includes all the best moments and highlights—from birth to her first steps to birthday parties, learning to ride a bike, and, more recently, her first piano recital. It's a wonderful way to keep the memories fresh and relive all the best moments of her life.

To be fair, that's more than I'd expect any father to do. It's very time-consuming and requires a lot of skill. I'm fortunate to have learned how to do it in college, and it serves as my artistic expression. I love doing it. But I mention it because, for me, it's a testament to the importance of those moments. More important than the video itself is the fact that I was there and present to record it. I was present at her birth, her first steps, and helping her ride a bike for the first time (with a GoPro strapped to my chest). You can be present in those moments. Whether or not you record them is up to you. But your child will remember you being there. Even when the memories fade, they'll know you were there. It'll be recorded in their subconscious as a feeling. My kid will have a video library of her most precious childhood memories to review for the rest of her life. But it's the moments that really count. Being there is an expression of your love. Without saying a word, being there for your kid says, "You are the most important thing in the world to me right now." The more you do that, the more valuable they feel. And the more valuable they feel, the more they'll believe they can accomplish great things in life. The more valuable they feel, the more likely they are to find friendship and love.

As I write this chapter, it's just after Valentine's Day. I received a wonderful card from my daughter in which she wrote, "*Thank you so much for playing games with me. Thank you so much for spending time with me. Thank you so much for taking me places. Thank you so much for being fun and for being funny. And thank you so much for being a great dad.*" Then she wrote, "*Don't ever change.*" Yeah, I got a little choked up when I read that because it means my daughter knows how incredibly important she is to me.

We currently have two adorable Australian Shepherds. They're young and energetic dogs, and they're constantly pawing at my leg and begging me to play with them. And often I do. But sometimes I'm busy, so I'll grab them a rawhide chew, and that'll keep them occupied for a while. But imagine doing that with your kid. They tug at your pant leg, wanting you to play with them, but instead, you hand them a lollipop—or, when they're older, a wad of cash. That's the Executive Dad's greatest mistake, and it leads to his greatest regret.

The next question is, "Do I want to be loved or resented?" Do you want your kids to feel warmth in their hearts for you, think of you fondly, talk about you fondly, and tell stories of what they did with you, the experiences you shared, the conversations you had, the hugs you gave them? Or do you want them to resent you for investing time in work instead of them or choosing to go on a golf trip instead of taking them someplace fun? What kind of legacy do you want to leave?

I know my answer to that question. My legacy is that my daughter will have no doubts about how much we love her. She will be confident in herself and her ability to find a good relationship partner. She won't fall prey to addictive behaviors because she won't need to escape anxiety or depression. She will have all the tools she needs to create her own abundant life. She'll have a more fulfilling life as a result of earning it herself rather than being handed an inheritance. Ideally, my daughter will raise her own kids similarly, enabling my grandkids and great-grandkids to grow up with loving parents who continue to prioritize spending time with them. I choose to leave a legacy of love.

I'm not saying I'm more virtuous than you. The only reason I'm choosing to live this way is that I've learned from those who came before me. I've heard too many stories about regret. I've learned from others' mistakes, and I'm encouraging you to learn from those same mistakes and avoid repeating them. It doesn't have to be that way for you. Whatever path you're on and whatever you may feel programmed to do, there's always time to change. And that time is now. You can begin to change today and be a better dad, a better husband, and even better in your career. When your life is balanced, your body is healthy, and you're rested, energized, and feeling good, you're mentally sharper, think more clearly, and make better choices. The truth is you can do anything you want with your life. The truth is you have agency and choice. Do you want your children to have a big inheritance and low self-esteem, or do you want them to have the confidence and strength to make their own way in life?

It's tempting to simply give. Giving is easier than teaching. It takes less time. If you are a millionaire or multimillionaire or on your way to being wealthy, it's easy to throw money at things. Sometimes I'm guilty of that. I'll throw money at problems rather than fix them myself. I'll pay my assistant to do something I don't want to spend time doing, or I'll pay a handyman to fix something broken in my home. But with my kid and my marriage, it's different. I'm not going to pay someone else to entertain my kid. I'm not going to pay someone else to spend time with my wife. It's against my morals and values. It's the wrong thing to do.

And frankly, I want to play that role myself. When I think about what success really means, to me, it means freedom. And freedom means being able to do what you want when you want. That's why I want you to redefine legacy. I want you to redefine success for yourself. My practice has evolved into a seven-figure business. I'm very proud of it. Most hypnotherapists never reach this level. But it could be an eight-figure business. If I were ambitious, it could be a nine-figure business. Maybe your business is an eight-figure or nine-figure, or who knows, maybe you're even a billionaire at this point. (I've heard billionaires like to read.) But to think that someone like me could have a child who's thriving, happy, independent, and confident, while the child of someone far wealthier and more successful could be depressed, anxious, lacking self-confidence, addicted to drugs, and involved in unhealthy relationships—doesn't that strike you as a tragedy? What a shame it would be if your child had less happiness and joy than mine, not because you lack the resources to give them a better life, but because you simply didn't use those resources more wisely.

The pursuit of wealth is about survival. But once you figure out how to survive, the goal needs to evolve. How do you maximize happiness for yourself and your family? Money can't buy it. *Time* and *love* create it.

I've always encouraged Sienna to interact with other human beings. From the time she was old enough to speak, I would whisper to her as we were leaving a restaurant, "Sienna, go say goodbye to everybody." She would walk up to each table on our way to the front door, smile, wave, and say, "Bye!" And people would smile and wave back at her. That may seem small and insignificant, but I knew I was conditioning her to be comfortable interacting with people—even those she didn't know—before she was old enough to question it or develop shyness. She even appreciates this as a 10-year-old. One night, I took her out for pizza, and she asked if she could have some water (it was self-service). I said, "Sure, why don't you go get it?"

She walked inside and came back out with a cup of water. She sat down and said, "Dad, thanks for teaching me to be confident talking to people."

I asked, "Why do you say that?"

She replied, "Well, I couldn't reach the cups, so I just went over and asked somebody who worked there, and they got a cup for me."

That may seem small, but it's a product of raising her purposefully to be independent and confident. She'd talked to people so many times, ordered her own food, and did things like that; she felt very comfortable asking for help. I got a little choked up. It's one thing to know you're helping your child; it's another to know they appreciate it.

As a child, I would have been scared to do that at 10. I have no memories of asking a stranger to help me with anything at that age. My parents loved me and did a great job raising me, but instilling confidence wasn't on their radar. No reasonable person would blame them for it. However, the fact that my daughter has the confidence to do that will open many doors for her in life.

One beautiful afternoon, when she was about 7 or 8, she went down the street to play with her friends. They played outside by the creek for about three or four hours. That night, as I was tucking her into bed, I asked, "How did it feel to play outside all afternoon instead of watching TV or staying inside?" Sometimes, I ask her questions to learn what she thinks. She thought about it before answering, and her response surprised me. She said, "More... alive?" Damn it, I got choked up again because it was the answer I didn't even realize I was hoping for. It's true. We feel more alive when we're active outside. I've always wanted her to understand the benefits of being outside and playing instead of watching screens and being passive. The fact that she really noticed it and actually felt more alive hit me in a powerful way.

There are other moments we've shared which illustrate the importance of simply being there with her. I've learned powerful tools through Neuro-Linguistic Programming (NLP®) that have been incredibly helpful with clients, specifically in helping them eliminate fears. On one occasion, as Sienna and I were driving to lunch, I had a chance to use one effective technique. She had recently watched the Netflix series *Wednesday*, inspired by a character from *The Addams Family*. The show was rated TV-14, and my kiddo was only nine when she watched it. It had some violent images and a scary monster that had given her bad dreams. When she thought about it, she still felt scared. When she told me that, I said, "Hey, kiddo, can you picture that monster in your mind right now?"

She said, "Yeah."

I said, "Put a clown nose on him."

Within seconds, she was laughing out loud. From that point forward, she couldn't think of the monster and feel afraid because every time she imagined it, she saw it with the clown nose. That's a simple example of a technique I use with clients, but it was effective in teaching her something that not only eliminated her fear but that she also used later on a friend dealing with her own scary thought.

I'm very proud of the first time Sienna sang in public. She had the confidence to sing at a restaurant in front of about 20 strangers. It happened on a whim when a former client invited her to sing with him after discovering she was taking singing lessons. She immediately said yes, practiced "Somewhere Over the Rainbow" for a couple of weeks, then showed up and sang in front of a live audience for the very first time. That would have terrified me or any other person I've met—to get up in front of a room full of strangers and sing for the very first time. Watching her perform, even though she was a little nervous, the feelings of pride my wife and I shared in that moment are almost impossible to describe.

We've had conversations about spending money. At the time of this writing, Sienna's into slime. It's a crazy phenomenon with kids. She watches YouTube videos about slime, makes slime in our basement, and orders all kinds of slime from various companies. She has her own bank account and kid-friendly credit card. Sometimes, she tries to decide what to buy with her money and what not to. There are times when she asks if she should spend $20 on a toy or save up for something bigger. Because I'm there with her and fully present, I can share what I tell clients and what I've learned. "Imagine, kiddo, it's a week from now, and you have the slime but $20 less in your bank account. Are you happy?" I taught her a simple strategy many adults use to make good financial decisions. As a result, she made a decision she didn't regret.

Recently, Sienna went to the mall with friends (kids still go to the mall, although it's rare). She told me how the other girls spent all their money, but she still had a lot left. She mentioned how they were disappointed to be broke when they saw something they liked even more! These are the things your child may never fully understand if you're too busy working. They have to learn all the lessons you're not there to teach the hard way. The more time you have with them, the more of your wisdom you can impart to them. They can benefit from your wisdom at a younger age and avoid repeating the mistakes you've made.

Sometimes, I even watch silly YouTube videos with her that she thinks are hilarious but which make me roll my eyes. But that's time I spend understanding what she's into, what she finds funny, and what makes her laugh while determining whether it's good for her to watch certain things. Sometimes, I check her phone, look at her text messages, and YouTube watch history to ensure good things are going into her brain and bad stuff is not.

As I mentioned previously, I have a reminder on my phone that every evening says, *"Remind Sienna about gratitude."* As I say good-night, I'll say, "Hey, kiddo, what are you grateful for today?" She's learned to respond not just by listing stuff she got that day but things like playing with our dogs and cats or having lunch with Mom and Dad. I'm helping her instill a habit of practicing gratitude because it's easy for kids (and adults) to get so used to their quality of life that they forget to appreciate it. Sienna is used to having two dogs and two cats. She's used to having a beautiful loft bed to sleep in every night. She's used to having all these wonderful comforts in life. Each night, I'm helping her create a habit that will help her remain happy no matter what level of comfort or affluence she experiences.

The more time you spend with your kids, the more you can teach them, and the better their lives will become. And you can do this in ways that all the money in the world cannot.

CONCLUSION

It's vital to think about your most precious resource: time. How you invest that time will have the most significant impact on your life and legacy. As an executive or entrepreneur, you know a thing or two about investing. You start investing in a 401(k), knowing it will pay off in the future. You invest in real estate knowing it will increase in value. You invest time in your work, knowing it will benefit the company and improve your quality of life. You've invested the time to read this book.

However, it has become evident to me that many Executive Dads neglect their health and family relationships to maximize their professional achievements. This results in specific negative consequences that increase in severity over time. I view this as a tragedy because many men are simply unaware of these potential consequences until it is too late to prevent them. Often, the very men who make these mistakes do so with good intent—they believe they are providing wealth and security for their families and loved ones.

I've been emphasizing the value of investing your time in your kids. While that sounds obvious, I want to give you specific examples from the perspective of a therapist who has worked with thousands of people for over 20 years. I've learned just how powerful our childhood experiences can be and the incredible significance those experiences have on us throughout our adult lives.

As a successful adult, you have knowledge to share with your kids that will help them succeed in life. The amount of time you spend with them will determine how much of that knowledge you can impart during their first 18 years. You will never have a better opportunity to do this than while they live under your roof. The sooner you take action, the more powerful an impact you will have on them.

Every word of advice matters. Every shared smile matters. Every time you play with them matters. Every hug matters. Every "I love you" matters. Every time you tuck them in bed matters. Every meal you share matters. Every time you show interest in what they're into (sports, music, toys)—it matters.

Consider how much it impacts your 401(k) if you start contributing at 20 years old rather than 25 or 30. That's a good metaphor for investing time in your kids. Investing early (between the ages of 0 and 10) will have a far greater impact than working 80 hours a week during those first ten years and then having more time to spend with them from ages 10 to 18.

All the studies show that those early years are the most important.

I've given you examples of things that negatively impact your kids —abuse, neglect, abandonment. As the proud father of a very happy and confident 11-year-old girl, I'd like to present you with some examples of things that will have positive impacts on your kids.

Every seemingly minor conversation and interaction can have an impact.

Ever since my daughter has been old enough to speak, I've encouraged her to interact with other people. I've given you other examples of seemingly small interactions with her that have resulted in significant positive impacts on her personal development and self-confidence.

Here is a practical list of things you can do that will have a positive impact on your kids:

- Give them your full attention and really listen to what they say.
- Talk to them when driving them around town.
- Share nuggets of wisdom without being pushy about it.
- Ask them questions to understand what they're thinking.
- Play with them regularly and be goofy with them.
- Play games you don't enjoy because it makes them happy.
- Expose them to the activities you love.
- Jump around on bounce houses and trampolines with them when they're young.
- Become the kind of person you want your child to either be or marry someday.

These investments of your time will produce the following returns:

- You'll create a stronger bond with them.
- They'll feel more confident in themselves.
- They'll know they're important to you.
- They'll be more likely to listen to your advice (i.e., they won't tune you out).
- They'll be more prepared for life's challenges.
- They'll be more likely to find and create healthy relationships.

- They'll be better parents to their own kids (your grandkids) someday.
- They'll be less likely to become addicted to alcohol, drugs, or food.
- You'll have more fun with them and be a happier person.
- You'll enjoy the greatest feeling of fulfillment known to humankind as they flourish.

There is something incredibly satisfying about witnessing your investment paying off. If you started your own business or helped another one grow as an executive, you know the satisfaction of reaping the rewards of all the blood, sweat, and tears. With your kids, the feeling of fulfillment is even more profound. When my 9-year-old daughter volunteered to introduce me at my live event, casually asking, "Hey, Dad, can I introduce you at your event on Sunday?" I knew that was a return on many years of investing time, love, and guidance in her.

When she performed the introduction, standing in front of a room full of adults she'd never met and having memorized every word, I couldn't stop smiling. It took me a few minutes to calm down as I began my talk! Watching Sienna's first piano recital, my wife and I beamed with pride as she played piece after piece with fluidity and grace—a product of more than five years of driving her to lessons, finding an amazing teacher, investing in a baby grand piano, reminding her to practice daily, and instilling in her the confidence to perform well.

Recently, moving into our new home in a new neighborhood, it was great watching her effortlessly make a dozen new friends with a natural confidence that she just needs to be herself. This kind of behavior would be easy to take for granted, but I really appreciate it because I've seen what happens to kids who don't get the love, support, and guidance they need. And I want you to have that same kind of fulfillment.

I'm sharing this because I had an epiphany several years ago. Reflecting on the work I'd done with children of Executive Dads and how much they'd suffered due to not having the dad they needed in their corner, I thought about how good Sienna had it—a lot of kids don't. I imagined a lonely young girl whose dad wasn't around to take her to lunch or jump on trampolines with her. I imagined an 8-year-old boy looking at the other kids' dads in the bleachers and wondering why his dad couldn't be there for his little league game. And yeah, I got a little choked up.

My goal is to help you. It's not just about your kids. It's about your right to enjoy life more fully. Remember how I promised to share with you my thoughts on those existential questions? You know, "What's the meaning of life?" and all that stuff? Well, I don't know anyone who thinks our purpose is to support a life filled with misery and absent joy. We all want to experience joy. We all want love, happiness, and human connection. So when I have to articulate the meaning of life, I describe it as "doing what you love with the people you love." And the people you love the most should be your wife and kids. But even beyond what you love to do, it's about doing what's *right*. You might prefer working to taking your kid to the park. But does that make it the right thing to do? Not if it results in a kid who feels unloved. Fulfillment comes from balance.

We all live for these special experiences. I figured this out many years ago when taking my first trip to France to visit a good friend. I'll never forget that trip. We bonded so much during those two weeks that he and his future wife felt more like family by the end of that trip. I knew that was something I wanted to do again, and it fueled my desire to become financially free and independent. But if you're too busy making money to spend time with the ones you love, it isn't working. There has to be some balance. You can't go full throttle

100% of the time. I know this sounds a bit like the mission statement from *Jerry Maguire,* in which Tom Cruise's character—a high-powered sports agent—wrote about the need to have "fewer clients" and make "less money." Spoiler alert: he was immediately fired. But that's not how it has to be.

You don't have to sacrifice your health or family to hold your spot at the top of the ladder. And you don't have to settle for earning less. It's possible to play the game smarter. It's possible to create more balance. You get to define what success means to you. You get to choose. Your time is yours alone to spend. No one else controls you. No one but you controls how you think, feel, or behave. You're the CEO of your life. You can use your knowledge and intelligence to run your life more effectively so that all elements of the Trinity are properly aligned—health, wealth, and relationships. When this happens, you'll run like a well-oiled machine.

You'll perform better at work. Your children will have a better role model. Your wife will be happier. You'll age more gracefully. You'll be around for all the weddings, birthday parties, and anniversaries. You'll be surrounded by people you love. Your life will be happier and more peaceful. You'll know you did it the right way. One day, many years from now, when you're sitting in a rocking chair reflecting on your life, you won't be wishing you spent more time with your kids. You won't be wondering if they might have turned out better if you'd been around more often. You won't be shelling out money for therapists and rehab centers. Instead, you'll be watching them thrive. You'll recall memories of experiences you shared with them and smile, knowing that you not only gave them the best opportunity to create a happy life but also enjoyed all those moments fully along the way.

Take it from me. I've heard the stories of executive men further along in life. I'm bringing this warning from the future to your doorstep and giving you the option to heed it or ignore it. I sincerely hope my words and stories have given you valuable insight. I hope you and your family benefit from these perspectives. If you need help getting your subconscious on board with these changes, you know where to find me. Executivedads.com would be a good place to start.

You're the boss. It's up to you to decide what to do with your life.

THANK YOU FOR READING MY BOOK!

DOWNLOAD YOUR FREE GIFTS

Just to say thanks for buying and reading my book,
I would like to give you a free gift.
The Secret to Winning the Game of Life—no strings attached!

Scan the QR Code Here:

SCAN ME

I appreciate your interest in my book and value your feedback as it helps me improve future versions of this book. I would appreciate it if you could leave your invaluable review on Amazon.com with your feedback.

Thank you!

www.ingramcontent.com/pod-product-compliance
Lightning Source LLC
Chambersburg PA
CBHW050510210326
41521CB00011B/2396